The State and Revolution

This title is one of a series published to commemorate the centenary of V. I. Lenin's death. The others are as follows:

Imperialism and the National Question, V. I. Lenin

Lenin's Childhood, Isaac Deutscher
The Lenin Scenario, Tariq Ali
Not by Politics Alone: The Other Lenin, edited
by Tamara Deutscher

The State and Revolution

The Marxist Theory of the State and the Tasks of the Proletariat in the Revolution

V. I. LENIN

Introduction by Antonio Negri
Introduction translated by Gregory Elliott

VERSO
London • New York

The text we have used in this edition was transcribed by Zodiac
and Brian Baggins and is available at marxists.org.

This paperback edition first published by Verso 2024
First published in English by International Publishers 1932
© Verso 2024
Introduction © Antonio Negri 2024

1 3 5 7 9 10 8 6 4 2

Verso

UK: 6 Meard Street, London W1F 0EG
US: 388 Atlantic Avenue, Brooklyn, NY 11217
versobooks.com

Verso is the imprint of New Left Books

ISBN-13: 978-1-80429-284-6
ISBN-13: 978-1-80429-287-7 (US EBK)
ISBN-13: 978-1-80429-286-0 (UK EBK)

British Library Cataloguing in Publication Data
A catalogue record for this book is available from the British Library

Library of Congress Cataloging-in-Publication Data
Names: Lenin, Vladimir Il'ich, 1870–1924, author. | Negri, Antonio, 1933-
  author of introduction.
Title: The state and revolution : the Marxist theory of the state and
the tasks of the proletariat in the revolution / V. I. Lenin ;
introduction by Antonio Negri ; introduction translated by Gregory Elliott.
Other titles: Gosudarstvo i revoliu͡tsii͡a. English
Description: New York : Verso, [2024] | Includes bibliographical references.
Identifiers: LCCN 2023029345 (print) | LCCN 2023029346 (ebook) |
ISBN 9781804292846 (paperback) | ISBN 9781804292877 (ebook) Subjects:
LCSH: Marx, Karl, 1818–1883. | Socialism. | State, The. | Revolutions.
Classification: LCC HX314 .L3528313 2024 (print) | LCC HX314
(ebook) | DDC 320.1--dc23/eng/20230706
LC record available at https://lccn.loc.gov/2023029345
LC ebook record available at https://lccn.loc.gov/2023029346

Typeset in Monotype Fournier by Hewer Text UK Ltd, Edinburgh
Printed and bound by CPI Group (UK) Ltd, Croydon CR0 4YY

CONTENTS

Introduction

Antonio Negri

I

When asked which book offers the best introduction to Marxism, I answer: *The State and Revolution* by Vladimir Ilyich Lenin.[1] Why? Because, if Marx is the brains of Marxism, Lenin is its body; and, for materialists, the brain too is located in the body. Marxism is not an economic theory, but a *critique* of political economy, where critique, first of all, signifies one's capacity for analysis by immersion in a chaotic, conflict-ridden world, materially dominated by bosses who exploit you and a sovereign who commands you. These relations – 'exploits you', 'commands you' – mean that such control involves your body: that is, the bodies, energy, passions and values of those who live and work on our planet. With *The State and Revolution*, Lenin places bodies within the daily struggle where economic demands and political passion, emancipatory effort and emancipatory power, are conjoined. In this initial approach, *The State and Revolution* signifies bodies in struggle against the materiality of capitalist control.

This connection reveals an initial meaning of Marxism as critique: it signifies being *within* political economy, remaining inside the complex of acts of exploitation and means of power (of capitalism and sovereignty), inside the indissoluble bond that makes of them a state. The state is the exploitation of the bodies of labourers and command over the brains of subjects. Revolution is the critique exercised by bodies against this exploitation and sovereign power.

Emerging from the inside, critique, at the same time, induces the power of the *against*. 'Against' signifies understanding how bodies can proceed against capital; hence it invites translating *Capital* – the inexhaustible book of Marxist critique – into the materialist experiment of a possible revolution. Because the 'within-against' conjugation follows, and determines, the materialist mutation of the set of bodies into classes and thus constitutes the red thread of subjectivation into class struggle. The pedagogy of Marxism, which is only *science* qua critique and only critique qua *subjectivation*, is planted on this peak of Lenin's discourse. It is not possible to be Marxist other than within the Leninist paradox of the totality and the partial viewpoint. And notice then how *Capital* comes, so to speak, to be subjectivated – which does not mean abandoned to the pleasures of a philology that is invariably curious and sometimes dissolute, or to the ceremonies of a rebellious dogmatism. Rather, it means re-articulated in its historical relationship with struggles, in the different technical and political compositions of the two classes. As Roman Rosdolsky noted, the initial plan of *Capital* envisaged a chapter on the state. Marx was unable to write it as the continuation of the great chapters of economic critique he had already composed. But, in his historical writings and interventions in the International, the people and parties it comprised, he sketched a theoretical framework. There Lenin adopted it, and imparted to it a musculature, with the experience of a victorious class struggle taking the place of unclear incidents and occasional volcanic party polemics. Here, 'subjectivation' assumes its true meaning, as pedagogy and also as the apex of the operative synthesis of the 'within and against' we have registered in the pages of *The State and Revolution*.

Within and against possibly suffice to put both *Capital* and Marx's historical writings into prose. But *The State and Revolution* goes much further. The revolution, Lenin says, has begun. Where are we going? What is the *beyond* we are striving towards? And, here, Lenin's subjective action twists towards reality, from utopia to science, from science to the concreteness of revolutionary force. It seems that we have returned to the beginning, and that enthusiasm for being located *within* and struggling *against* capital has matured as such in a perpetual motion. Such is not the case: here subjectivation makes it possible positively to itemize the transitions that 'revolutionary deeds' must accomplish in order to construct the *beyond*, in order to go *beyond the beyond*, from socialism to communism. And the road is mapped out with the intelligence and power of *constituent praxis*.

Utopia is connected with reality and takes shape in conjunction with the attack on current class domination. Thus, the utopian 'withering away of the state' is understood in materialist terms as a *constituent process*. And we see this process completed, because it is no longer an ideal but a test for the subjectivity that transforms the real: Marx and Lenin are definitively recomposed – and with what force! Destroying the state and reconstructing the set of institutions that make a free existence possible become tasks accomplished in common. When we finish reading *The State and Revolution*, our bodies are engaged in that task.

II

The preface to the first edition of *The State and Revolution* is dated August 1917 and the 'Postscript to the First Edition' is dated 30 November. According to the latter,

> This pamphlet was written in August and September 1917. I had already drawn up the plan for the next, the seventh, chapter, 'The Experience of the Russian Revolutions of 1905 and 1917'. Apart from the title, however, I had no time to write a single line of the chapter; I was 'interrupted' by a political crisis – the eve of the October revolution of 1917. Such an 'interruption' can only be welcomed; but the writing of the second part of the pamphlet ('The Experience of the Russian Revolutions

of 1905 and 1917') will probably have to be put off for a long time. It is more pleasant and useful to go through the 'experience of the revolution' than to write about it.

So, the book was born inside the revolution, in August– September 1917 (when, following an initial unsuccessful attempt at insurrection in July, Lenin was compelled to flee Moscow). In composing it, Lenin used his notes on 'Marxism and the State', written in Switzerland in the period immediately preceding his return to Russia. In Switzerland, where he had been forced to seek refuge from Kraków, then in Austrian Poland, which refused Russian citizens residence after the outbreak of war, Lenin wrote a triple series of texts. The first was a set of philosophical studies, collected in the notebooks on Hegel; the second was devoted to the study of imperialism and was to become his popular essay on the subject; finally, there were the notebooks on 'Marxism and the State' which represent the immediate antecedent to August 1917.

We have already seen that the opuscule came to a halt at the seventh chapter. As regards the preceding chapters, Lenin offered a general overview of definitions of class society and the state in Chapter 1. In Chapter 2, he reconstructed this concept from Marx's writings on the 1848 revolutions. Chapter 3 was devoted to the experience of the Paris Commune of 1871 and Marx's analysis of it. Chapter 4 contains additional explanations and follows the writings of Marx, and especially Engels, in the polemic with German social democracy (in particular, Lenin takes up the critiques of the Erfurt and Gotha programmes). In Chapter 5, Lenin directly tackles the problem of the 'withering away of the state' and defines the material bases for this process. Chapter 6 contains a further ferocious attack on Georgi Plekhanov and Karl Kautsky – in short, on the social-democratic opportunism of the Second International. Of Chapter 7, as noted, only the plan exists.

In a sense, the outline of *The State and Revolution* is pedagogical enough, proceeding from recuperation of Engels's hypotheses on the origins of the state and analysing the maturation in Marx of a class standpoint, nourished by the experience of the struggles of 1848 and 1871. The discourse then switches to the communist programme and confronts the positions of the parties of the Second International, polemicizing with social-democratic reformism regarded as opportunism. The original plan envisaged, in conclusion, an analysis of the experience of the 1917 Revolution, in order to affirm the actuality of the communist programme and demonstrate its mass maturity. But, at this point, Chapter 7 is missing. Let us read its outline in full:

1 New 'popular creation' in the Revolution. *Quid est?* (Plekhanov, 1906). 2 Lessons of 1905 (resolutions of the Mensheviks and Bolsheviks, 1906). 3 Eve of the 1917 Revolution: theses of October 1905. 4 Experience of 1917. Rise of mass movement, Soviets (their scope and weakness; dependency of the petty bourgeoisie. 5 Prostitution of the Soviets by the Socialist Revolutionaries and

Mensheviks: militia, armed people; military section, the 'sections'; economic section; exploration of 3–5 July; 'independence' of the power of party organizations. 6 The Kornilov episode: degeneration of the Mensheviks and Socialist Revolutionaries; the negotiation of 14–19 September. 7 'Messianism'. *Who will begin?*

Even today, rereading this conclusion makes one shiver at the incredible foresight and enormous force conveyed by this *incipit*.

III

However, a reader unaccustomed to studying the class struggle might get the impression from these brief mentions of the history of the text (internal to its composition) that it was, as it were, occasional, tactical. Evidence of this would be the fact that the text amasses references to the Marxist tradition in order to polemicize against social-democratic revisionism and the forces opposed at the time to the advance of the revolution. The occasional character of the essay would take precedence over its radicalism. Viewed thus, we are dealing with the continuation of an ideological battle bound up with the specific location of the Bolshevik Party in the Socialist International. The text is indeed consistent with earlier polemics and theoretical clashes, resuming and developing their themes. The battle against Plekhanov rests on the battle against Kautsky, and it, in turn, on Engels's firm rejection of the Erfurt Programme as well as Marx's of the Gotha

Programme, and so on and so forth. From this perspective, it would not be mistaken to regard the text as a tactical, ideological weapon – or to put it another way, it does not convey truth and invention.

But to read it exclusively in this light is seriously inadequate. For what makes *The State and Revolution* a classical text of political thought is not the repetition of the critique of social chauvinism, but – at a crucial moment, in the heat of insurrection – a destructive critique of the very concept of the state and the foundation of a different concept of *power*, with greetings to all those who for more than a century have repeated that Marxism lacks a doctrine of the state.

Let us see, then, how this project unfolds in Lenin's thinking in a dramatic, dawning situation. On the one hand, the concept of the state is isolated from the powers it arrogates to itself as general organizer and motor of the functioning of society. The administrative and productive functions the state machine claims to comprise and nurture can be stripped from its definition. Already in the Paris Commune, these functions had been absorbed and expressed in new institutional forms of the social, rather than being subordinate bodies or apparatuses of state power. This was fundamental for communists, who seek to 'convert . . . the state from an organ superimposed on society into one completely subordinate to it' (as Marx stresses in his critique of the Gotha Programme). Thus is outlined a kind of *way up*, following the dynamics of the functioning of society, which is shot through by the forces of labour in struggle as they demolish the state (or 'political power, properly so called', in the splendid definition offered by *The Poverty of Philosophy*). This is the projected road of *dual power*, which is not a tactical indication for the revolutionary movement (it is also, but not only, that at this point, on the path from insurrection to revolution, as we shall shortly see). It is a definition, ontological in its import, of how the state is composed and of what: it is always a power defined by a *balance of antagonistic forces*, triumphant for the owners of capital in its current form, but headed for destruction with the victory of the proletarian class struggle. And this is only a start. From the victory against the state, the working class and the labouring classes must find the way to construct a new society; they will have to do so concurrently with the dynamic of the destruction of the capitalist state. They will dismantle it, making the exercise of working-class democracy the key to the process. In this way Lenin liquidates the anarchism that does not think beyond the destruction of the state to the organized reconstruction of the social.

The *way down*, from revolutionary victory to the construction of a socialist society and, at the same time, the establishment of the premises of communism, will likewise be invested by class struggle in the form of dual power. Proletarian dual power, taking possession of the state, initiates the class struggle to destroy it and, simultaneously, projects the construction of a different society, a different order where equality and liberty (ceasing to be formal) become real.

But here, those who regard *The State and Revolution* as a tactical, occasional text, might object that, while Lenin theorized a dual conception of power and the state, he defined dual power as a brief episode, an expedient useful only at the height of the revolutionary process. And, indeed, when we read the pages on dual power in *The State and Revolution*, it seems that urgency and enthusiasm in making the revolution prevail over a materialist analysis of the state: dual power seems to be a theoretical and practical weapon in the immediate confrontation, and of temporary, transient use. But this is not the case. The subsumption of dual power into a tactical category is purely rhetorical. There is no doubt that this scrap of argumentation unbalances the theoretical analysis, undermines its ontological texture. And of course, readers might be troubled by how captivating – even in Vladimir Ilyich – the experience of the revolutionary event can be, exalting in the 'deed' and taking pride in the victorious moment . . . to the point of setting theory aside. Not actually disavowing it – because theory (of dual power in particular) is an accumulation of revolutionary temporality, of experiences of victory and defeat – is what remains essential in the knowledge of power and therefore in the conduct of the revolutionary process. And Lenin knows it.

IV

Constructing a different social order: revolution consists in this, and it is this spirit that runs through *The State and*

Revolution. But a spirit that has been disowned and betrayed! In fact, if the 'way up' has been acknowledged by all and respected by communists, the 'way down' – the proposal of the 'withering away of the state' – has been very much under-appreciated. The reluctance to read it for what it is – a proposal to deepen the class struggle *within*, *against* and *beyond* the conquest of the state – is incredible. On the part of the bourgeoisie, it has been asked how a revolutionary and intellectual of Lenin's stature could have articulated such utopian idiocy – the withering away, the end, of the state. On the part of so-called Leninists, it is repeated that the 'withering away of the state' does not signify its end, its term, but indicates what would follow the creation of a classless society which, in its turn, cannot be constructed other than by maximum reinforcement of the state (and the class struggle) in the dictatorship of the proletariat. This is what Stalin wrote in *Problems of Leninism*: 'Some comrades interpreted the thesis on . . . the withering away of the state to mean . . . a justification of the counterrevolutionary theory that the class struggle is subsiding and that state power is to be relaxed . . . The state will wither way, not as a result of a relaxation of the state power, but as a result of its utmost consolidation.' At this point, debate was at an end. To liberals scandalized by the 'dictatorship of the proletariat', Stalinists retorted: 'Your state too is nothing but a dictatorship – the dictatorship of capital, of the bourgeoisie.' So: dictatorship *vs* dictatorship; and the most dubious interpreters have concluded: 'Fascism = Communism; Hitler = Lenin'.

One thing is certain: Lenin is far removed from this tragic quarrel. The withering away of the state is not utopia, nor is it the dictatorial constipation of the revolutionary process. It is the labour of constructing a *different power*: it is the constituent motor of the class struggle set in motion at the very moment of the insurrectionary clash, which consists in institutionalizing the organs of insurrection, giving institutional form to the antagonistic figures who empty the state of its force. The soviets of peasants in arms, for example, strip the state both of its 'regalian' capacity to lead the nation in arms and of the 'force of law' in guaranteeing and protecting landed property, by means of the Tsar's Cossack force. (Thereby unmasked is the mystery of the link between legality and efficacy that so absorbs juridical science in the so-called *Rechtsstaat*: in this paradigmatic instance, the 'rational' shell of the two terms is none other than the Tsar!) On the one side, then, the class enemy is stripped of its weapons; on the other, with weapons and peasant agreement in the soviets, new institutions of common ownership and cooperative production for those hitherto always deprived of them are constructed. This is only one example and could be multiplied a thousand times: a historical power has been freed, resulting in a new system of right through the constituent exercise of proletarian force and articulating abolition of the state and construction of a new order.

'Withering away': self-professed Leninists still tell us that it signifies survival and institutional accumulation; of course, provided it is seen in positivist terms, in accordance with the lifeless materialism for which there is no room in Lenin, because, for him, 'withering away' is the exaltation of invariably productive insurrectionary subjectivation, which must always remain living. Superficially, Lenin warns, 'dual power' withers away rapidly and must be given free rein when the possibility of it presents itself (as in February 1917 and again in October 1917). Later, in the post-revolutionary process of socialist construction, it will be possible to revive this dual power, bring to the fore its profound dimension and extract from it the same force as in the insurrectionary process. There is nothing 'automatic', nothing 'spontaneous', about this 'withering away', as in any other process of accumulation. There is mass subjectivation and the action of mass vanguards, articulation of their differences, and construction in common. Duality of power is thus exercised as permanent *constituent power*.

One last note on the equation of fascism and Leninism as similar forms of totalitarian government by theoreticians of 'totalitarianism'. Let us grant this denunciation, recalling that power is always an open relationship. Now, on this basis, in their form, fascism and Leninism could indeed represent two similar figures of totalitarian seizure of state power. Nevertheless, ontologically different (and irreducible to the other) is the state in the hands of capitalists confronting a revolution that eradicates capitalism (and with it the state) from control of the totality; which, in fact, proceeds in such a way as to construct another, opposed reality, the concrete totality of freedom. The latter is the programme of *The State and Revolution*.

V

Of course, we cannot say that *The State and Revolution* is a text that has not been read and studied. Yet, for the majority of its readers, it continues to pertain to the realm of myth, rather than that of rational politics – that is to say, an episode bound up with the exceptional moment ('magical' for some, 'cursed' for others) represented by the passage of the October Revolution. Hence the signature, the seal, of Lenin on this passage.

Let us note that authors who regard *The State and Revolution* as a 'mythical' text pertain to right and left alike. On the right, *The State and Revolution* has been hypothesized as the manifesto of the 'secret of power', revealed by a political decision that renders Lenin's akin to the sublime production of the metaphysical Übermensch. But, without dredging up such extremes (which delight the ideologues of the extreme right), there is no doubt that, even for more academic authors – hence the expression of mainstream Western political science (one thinks, for example, of Max Weber or Carl Schmitt) – Lenin's thinking on the state and revolution can be described as the 'irrational' moment of 'political rationality', the founding 'decision' confronted with administrative rationality, and, as such, is paradigmatic in the theory of power. Were this theoretical absorption of Lenin into the classical doctrine of the modern state to be right, however, we should have to conclude that the Marxist critique of Hegelian public law was incorrect – that is, it did not sufficiently demystify the irrationality in command by the state, recognizing it as an accumulation of expropriation and alienation of productive forces. Thus, along with Marx, Lenin might still be assimilated to bourgeois *Staatslehre*. However, this abstract deduction, this reactionary syllogism is contradicted by the fact that Lenin made the revolution and expounded the ontology of power (dual power) in the full light of day, verified it scientifically, with indelible concreteness.

But the objection (addressed to mainstream interpreters) of not grasping the specificity of Lenin's conception of power and its overthrow is also directed against some of his readers on the left, who, in disguised form, take up the same complementarity of the rational and irrational claimed by reactionary authors. Thus (to stick to proximate references), in the psychoanalytical implications of Hegel's Master–Bondsman dialectic (for Slavoj Žižek), or in the symbolic productivity of an event assumed as an historical over-determination (Alain Badiou), the political action invoked by Leninism finds itself translated into the agency of an irrationality, secreted in every form of power and now suddenly unveiled and victorious. There is something ignoble about these readings of *The State and Revolution*: the long shadow of Nietzsche becomes reactionary in this figure of the dialectic that is resolved merely in mystified, mythical terms; as if revolution, or rather the decision to rise up, were an orgasm, and not – as it was for Lenin – a prolonged labour of preparation, an exacting laboratory experiment, and a protracted project inasmuch as the revolution is continuous, permanent, up until the construction of communism. From the *Letters from Afar* to the *April Theses* to *The State and Revolution*, Lenin works to give shape to the machine of revolution, of conquest of the state through soviets, to which are entrusted the democratic, productive articulation of the 'dictatorship of the proletariat'.

So is there a theory of the state in *The State and Revolution*, organized by the strict mutual implication of insurrection, constituent power, dictatorship of the proletariat, withering away of the state? Of the 'dictatorship of the proletariat' as constituent power wherein the revolution can be fully realized? In my view, yes – contrary to the denial of some major bourgeois theoreticians, such as Norberto Bobbio, and despite the reluctant acknowledgement by others (for example, in Hans Kelsen). This affirmation of mine is based on the firmness and continuity of the sober constitutive mechanisms at work in *The State and Revolution* and Lenin's other writings, at least until the New Economic Policy – and their constitutional effects.

But there is realization and there is realization, and they are not equally valid. As we have seen, Stalin was intent on being the most thoroughgoing realizer of the Leninist system. If we read his *Problems of Leninism*, we find corroborating evidence of this: the dictatorship of the proletariat is the road – the only viable one – to building socialism. This conception prevailed, with the tragic consequences with which we are familiar. This was a practice, indisputably statist, of constituted power, not a process of constituent power. Many were the communists who opposed Stalin, even in the juridical field – Evgeny Pashukanis, in the first instance, and so many others. They were ruled out of order, but their critique continued to be present in the communist movement. And it is certain, for example, that a dialectical critique was operative in the thought and action of Mao Zedong from the 1930s until the Cultural Revolution, which sought constituent endeavour in the hands of the revolutionary masses/classes open to the construction of the new China. The lesson drawn by Mao from Lenin's *Philosophical Notebooks*, in the two texts *On Contradiction* and *On Practice* from 1936, is wholly directed to positing the theoretical premises for a constituent dynamic of communist revolution. What, exactly, are we talking about? A theory of constituent power which, from *The State and Revolution*, opens out onto the affirmation of liberty and equality, constructing collective structures that democratically strip the state of the functions entrusted it by capital for the reproduction of society, and which instead produce institutions of the commons.

And will there be a 'residue of the state', of violence geared to domination that might be abstract, but which will continue to ensure (also forcibly) the functioning of the whole machine? According to Lenin, this residue should spontaneously disappear and will do so when the development of the class struggle has swept the globe and developed communism as a productive system, finally freeing humanity from the need to toil in order to live! A political and technological dream? Certainly: a dream shared in common by the Marx of the *Grundrisse* and the Lenin of *The State and Revolution*. And it is impressive to see how Lenin posits as conditions for the withering away of the state more or less the same dispositions that tell of the triumph of the 'general intellect' in the *Grundrisse*: first, the elimination of the distinction between manual and mental labour; second, the full development of the productive forces; and finally – a third material condition already included in the first and second – the anticipation of a qualitative leap that transforms the productive forces – in other words, a change in the consciousness and body of workers. Only on this basis does the withering away of the state become possible for Lenin. A dream? Yes – but also a project. Permanent revolution lives off this project and is built on its warp and weft.

In *The State and Revolution*, Lenin refers to the withering away of the state (the ultimate disappearance of an 'indisputably' political power) as a pathway based on *habituation* to democracy – that is, the continuous exercise of a power from below that constructs institutions of the commons. This image might seem utopian, but only to those who entertain a theological idea of the state or, at any rate, are convinced of its ontological necessity. In fact, they speak of custom without any qualms, assuming it as the source of law, and have no hesitation in basing the efficacy of processes of legitimation of power on it and, if needs be, moulding the consensus obtained by minority fractions in society into entitlement to command based on a transcendental will. Or even, in secular societies, transforming the will of an electoral majority into the 'general will' – representative of people and nation – usurping the power of singularities and stripping them of differences, reducing what is plural and rich in possibilities to unity. In order to avoid these ideological blunders, it suffices to reread Lenin's pages on the Hegelian dialectic (in the *Philosophical Notebooks*, which are contemporaneous with his reflection on the Marxist theory of the state) to understand what is meant by 'habit' in Lenin's language. It means mass behaviour that becomes institutions; and this 'becoming' signifies 'generating', encouraging, constituting, innovating, stripping the dialectic of the idealist illusion of 'reversing to preserve', of 'developing by integrating', which Hegelianism (and why not also Hegel?) proposed to the political thought of the victorious bourgeoisie. The historical materialism of Lenin (and Marx and Mao) plays on dialectical passion not in order to facilitate the idealist and individualist imbroglio of the subjection of motion to crude *Wirklichkeit*, but so as to nourish the proletarian accumulation of power in subsequent extensions and massifications, including ruptures in, and deviations from, the process. *The State and Revolution* is a door that opens for political thinking beyond modernity.

VI

Through this door passed the socialist and anti-colonial revolutions of the twentieth century, Asian, South American and African. Lenin defined these struggles as *anti-imperialist*. The Leninist subjectivation of Marx's concept of the working class made it possible to enhance its power and transform the alliance of variously exploited social strata into confluence and aggregation, into a convergence of struggles against the institutions of exploitation and the social layers benefiting from it. This planetary perspective reconfigured the struggle as anti-imperialist, extending the concept of the working class adopted by Lenin (and Marx before him) as vector of the international political recomposition of the subordinate. It further anticipated the development that would lead to the *intersection* of emancipatory struggles and the *convergence* of liberation struggles. An enormous panorama of struggles thus opens up for those who wish to read *The State and Revolution* as projecting its apparatus onto the 'long twentieth century' and its sequel. And all this under the sign of primordial Marxism – that of the *Communist Manifesto*.

In fact, Lenin's anti-imperialism forms the weft of a *reinforced* internationalism. In other words, Marx's internationalism is taken up by Lenin in radical fashion here: the revolutionary relationship is sculpted as *agency* that overcomes the limits of any nationalism and opens the revolutionary struggle out onto its global dimensions. Once again, this is a space of which the thinking of modernity, from Immanuel Kant to Hannah Arendt, has only skimmed the surface in vague proposals for 'perpetual peace' or 'cosmopolitan spirit'.

However, in this instance, once again, on right and left alike, Leninist internationalism has been attacked and its concept negated, on the grounds that it itself was centralizing and imperialist. On the contrary, for Lenin, internationalism is not in contradiction with the right of peoples to determine their own free destiny. In no instance does it deny, but rather insists, on solving the difficulties and overcoming the obstacles that impede conferring institutional form on a people in a territory, on a nation in its environment. This incitement is not contradictory. In fact, Lenin urges the construction of internationalism precisely by stressing the power of its components. Now, strong opposition to Leninist internationalism was to arise not only on the right, from the nationalist impudence that bases its strength on conserving the past, in identitarian fanaticism and racism. From within the Third International steered by Bolshevism, this internationalism would often be characterized as inadequate and incapable of developing the communist programme. And the new world configured by Lenin's thought and action would fall victim to clashes and crises in which the nationalistic, reactionary consequences of 'socialism in one country' stood out ever more clearly.

Even so, Leninist internationalism has withstood these injuries and perversions. It still represents a living moment, a beating heart, in any project to reconstruct a communist movement. If we ask why, we shall immediately appreciate that the reason for the vitality of Lenin's internationalism

consists in the fact that, for him, 'international', before referring to nations, refers to a vector of politics that became
central in the twentieth century: *mass subjectivation*. For
Lenin, internationalism functions with reference to a global
subject, enhancing its image, developing its impact, its power.
For Lenin, the political experience of the masses, the multitude, stands at the base of any communist political project.
Hence, internationalism does not simply mean action that
inhabits and articulates multiple spatial dimensions, but the
action that invests them, involving 'the consciousness,
the will, the passions, the imagination of thousands of
people . . . of many tens of millions of people spurred on by
the most bitter class struggle'. Internationalism signifies
a multitude of revolutionary subjects, but also indicates
that any consciousness is activated by a multitude of cooperative relations and subversive passions: mass subjectivation
on the global terrain of this world of ours that is to be revo-
lutionized. Already, in *The State and Revolution*, Lenin had
grasped – what tremendous anticipation! – that the mass
engaged in the process of liberation from the chains of capitalism had challenged the very existence of the state, the
essence of sovereignty, the concept of capital. All at once,
globally.

VII

So *The State and Revolution* is a classic of political thought.
Not of modern political thinking, producer of the concept of

the sovereign state, but of a political thought that continuously approximates to the idea of the withering away of the state, in whose stead will be laid the foundations for a rich production of institutions of the commons.

September 2022
Translated by Gregory Elliott

Bibliography

Althusser, Louis, 'Lenin and Philosophy' (1968), trans. Ben Brewster, in *Lenin and Philosophy & Other Essays*, London: New Left Books, 1971.

Bobbio, Norberto, *Which Socialism?* (1976), ed. Richard Bellamy and trans. Roger Griffin, Cambridge: Polity Press, 1986.

Budgen, Sebastian, Kouvelakis, Stathis and Žižek, Slavoj, eds, *Lenin Reloaded: Towards a Politics of Truth*, Durham, NC and London: Duke University Press, 2007.

Lenin, V. I., 'The State and Revolution: The Marxist Theory of the State and the Tasks of the Proletariat in the Revolution' (1917), in *Collected Works*, Vol. 25, Moscow: Progress Publishers, 1964.

Lukács, György, *Lenin: A Study on the Unity of his Thought* (1924), trans. Nicholas Jacobs, London: New Left Books.

Negri, Antonio, *Factory of Strategy: Thirty-Three Lessons on Lenin* (1973), trans. Arianna Bové, New York: Columbia University Press, 2014.

Schmitt, Carl, *The Concept of the Political* (1932), trans. George Schwab, Chicago and London: University of Chicago Press, 2007.

Stalin, J., 'The Results of the First Five-Year Plan' (1933), in *Problems of Leninism*, Moscow: Foreign Languages Publishing House, 1953.

Zolo, Danilo, *La Teoria comunista dell'estinzione dello Stato*, Bari: De Donato, 1974.

PREFACE TO THE FIRST EDITION

The question of the state is now acquiring particular importance both in theory and in practical politics. The imperialist war has immensely accelerated and intensified the process of transformation of monopoly capitalism into state-monopoly capitalism. The monstrous oppression of the working people by the state, which is merging more and more with the all-powerful capitalist associations, is becoming increasingly monstrous. The advanced countries – we mean their hinterland – are becoming military convict prisons for the workers.

The unprecedented horrors and miseries of the protracted war are making the people's position unbearable and increasing their anger. The world proletarian revolution is clearly maturing. The question of its relation to the state is acquiring practical importance.

The elements of opportunism that accumulated over the decades of comparatively peaceful development have given rise to the trend of social-chauvinism which dominated the official socialist parties throughout the world. This trend – socialism in words and chauvinism in deeds (Plekhanov, Potresov, Breshkovskaya, Rubanovich and, in a slightly veiled form, Tsereteli, Chernov and Co. in Russia; Scheidemann, Legien, David and others in Germany; Renaudel, Guesde and Vandervelde in France and Belgium; Hyndman and the Fabians in England, etc., etc.)[1] – is conspicuous for the base, servile adaptation of the 'leaders of socialism' to the interests not only of 'their' national bourgeoisie, but of 'their' state, for the majority of the so-called Great Powers have long been exploiting and enslaving a whole number of small and weak nations. And the imperialist war is a war for the division and redivision of this kind of booty. The struggle to free the working people from the influence of the bourgeoisie in general, and of the imperialist bourgeoisie in particular, is impossible without a struggle against opportunist prejudices concerning the 'state'.

First of all, we examine the theory of Marx and Engels of the state, and dwell in particular detail on those aspects of this theory which are ignored or have been distorted by the opportunists. Then we deal specially with the one who is chiefly responsible for these distortions, Karl Kautsky,[2] the best-known leader of the Second International (1889–1914), which has met with such miserable bankruptcy in the present war. Lastly, we sum up the main results of the experience of the Russian revolutions of 1905 and particularly of 1917. Apparently, the latter is now (early August 1917) completing the first stage of its development; but this revolution as a whole can only be understood as a link in a chain of socialist proletarian revolutions being caused by the imperialist war. The question of the relation of the socialist proletarian revolution to the state, therefore, is acquiring not only practical political importance, but also the significance of a most urgent problem of the day, the problem of explaining to the masses what they will have to do before long to free themselves from capitalist tyranny.

The Author
August 1917

PREFACE TO THE SECOND EDITION

The present, second edition is published virtually unaltered, except that section 3 has been added to Chapter 2.

The Author
Moscow
17 December 1918

1

CLASS SOCIETY AND THE STATE

I. The State: A Product of the Irreconcilability of Class Antagonisms

What is now happening to Marx's theory has, in the course of history, happened repeatedly to the theories of revolutionary thinkers and leaders of oppressed classes fighting for emancipation. During the lifetime of great revolutionaries, the oppressing classes constantly hounded them, received their theories with the most savage malice, the most furious hatred and the most unscrupulous campaigns of lies and slander. After their death, attempts are made to convert them into harmless icons, to canonize them, so to say, and to hallow their *names* to a certain extent for the 'consolation' of the oppressed classes and with the object of duping the latter, while at the same time robbing the revolutionary theory of its *essence*, blunting its revolutionary edge and vulgarizing it. Today, the bourgeoisie and the opportunists within the labour movement concur in this doctoring of Marxism. They omit, obscure, or distort the revolutionary side of this theory, its revolutionary soul. They push to the foreground and extol what is or seems acceptable to the bourgeoisie. All the social-chauvinists are now 'Marxists' (don't laugh!). And more and more frequently German bourgeois scholars, only yesterday specialists in the annihilation of Marxism, are speaking of the 'national-German' Marx, who, they claim, educated the labour unions which are so splendidly organized for the purpose of waging a predatory war!

In these circumstances, in view of the unprecedently wide-spread distortion of Marxism, our prime task is to *re-establish* what Marx really taught on the subject of the state. This will necessitate a number of long quotations from the works of Marx and Engels themselves. Of course, long quotations will render the text cumbersome and not help at all to make it popular reading, but we cannot possibly dispense with them. All, or at any rate all the most essential passages in the works of Marx and Engels on the subject of the state must by all means be quoted as fully as possible so that the reader may form an independent opinion of the totality of the views of the founders of scientific socialism, and of the evolution of those views, and so that their distortion by the 'Kautskyism' now prevailing may be documentarily proved and clearly demonstrated.

Let us begin with the most popular of Engels's works, *The Origin of the Family, Private Property and the State*, the sixth edition of which was published in Stuttgart as far back as 1894. We have to translate the quotations from the

German originals, as the Russian translations, while very numerous, are for the most part either incomplete or very unsatisfactory.

Summing up his historical analysis, Engels says:

> The state is, therefore, by no means a power forced on society from without; just as little is it 'the reality of the ethical idea', 'the image and reality of reason', as Hegel maintains. Rather, it is a product of society at a certain stage of development; it is the admission that this society has become entangled in an insoluble contradiction with itself, that it has split into irreconcilable antagonisms which it is powerless to dispel. But in order that these antagonisms, these classes with conflicting economic interests, might not consume themselves and society in fruitless struggle, it became necessary to have a power, seemingly standing above society, that would alleviate the conflict and keep it within the bounds of 'order'; and this power, arisen out of society but placing itself above it, and alienating itself more and more from it, is the state.
>
> (sixth German edition, pp. 177–8)[1]

This expresses with perfect clarity the basic idea of Marxism with regard to the historical role and the meaning of the state. The state is a product and a manifestation of the *irreconcilability* of class antagonisms. The state arises where, when and insofar as class antagonism objectively *cannot* be reconciled. And, conversely, the existence of the state proves that the class antagonisms are irreconcilable.

It is on this most important and fundamental point that the distortion of Marxism, proceeding along two main lines, begins.

On the one hand, the bourgeois, and particularly the petty-bourgeois, ideologists, compelled under the weight of indisputable historical facts to admit that the state only exists where there are class antagonisms and a class struggle, 'correct' Marx in such a way as to make it appear that the state is an organ for the reconciliation of classes. According to Marx, the state could neither have arisen nor maintained itself had it been possible to reconcile classes. From what the petty-bourgeois and philistine professors and publicists say, with quite frequent and benevolent references to Marx, it appears that the state does *reconcile* classes. According to Marx, the state is an organ of class rule, an organ for the *oppression* of one class by another; it is the creation of 'order', which legalizes and perpetuates this oppression by moderating the conflict between classes. In the opinion of the petty-bourgeois politicians, however, order means the reconciliation of classes, and not the oppression of one class by another; to alleviate the conflict means reconciling classes and not depriving the oppressed classes of definite means and methods of struggle to overthrow the oppressors.

For instance, when, in the revolution of 1917, the question of the significance and role of the state arose in all its magnitude as a practical question demanding immediate action, and, moreover, action on a mass scale, all the Socialist-Revolutionaries and Mensheviks descended at once to the petty-bourgeois theory that the 'state' 'reconciles' classes.[2] Innumerable resolutions and articles by politicians of both these parties are thoroughly saturated with this petty-bourgeois and philistine 'reconciliation' theory. That the state is an organ of the rule of a definite class which *cannot* be reconciled with its antipode (the class opposite to it) is something the petty-bourgeois democrats will never be able to understand. Their attitude to the state is one of the most striking manifestations of the fact that our Socialist-Revolutionaries and Mensheviks are not socialists at all (a point that we Bolsheviks have always maintained), but petty-bourgeois democrats using near-socialist phraseology.

On the other hand, the 'Kautskyite' distortion of Marxism is far more subtle. 'Theoretically', it is not denied that the state is an organ of class rule, or that class antagonisms are irreconcilable. But what is overlooked or glossed over is this: if the state is the product of the irreconcilability of class antagonisms, if it is a power standing *above* society and '*alienating* itself *more and more* from it', it is clear that the liberation of the oppressed class is impossible not only without a violent revolution, *but also without the destruction* of the apparatus of state power which was created by the ruling class and which is the embodiment of this 'alienation'. As we shall see later, Marx very explicitly drew this theoretically self-evident conclusion on the strength of a concrete historical analysis of the tasks of the revolution. And – as we shall show in detail further on – it is this conclusion which Kautsky has 'forgotten' and distorted.

II. Special Bodies of Armed Men, Prisons, etc.

Engels continues:

> As distinct from the old gentile [tribal or clan] order, the state, first, divides its subjects according to territory . . .³

This division seems 'natural' to us, but it costs a prolonged struggle against the old organization according to generations or tribes.

> The second distinguishing feature is the establishment of a public power which no longer directly coincides with the population organizing itself as an armed force. This special, public power is necessary because a self-acting armed organization of the population has become impossible since the split into classes . . . This public power exists in every state; it consists not merely of armed men but also of material adjuncts, prisons, and institutions of coercion of all kinds, of which gentile [clan] society knew nothing . . .

Engels elucidates the concept of the 'power' which is called the state, a power which arose from society but places itself above it and alienates itself more and more from it. What does this power mainly consist of? It consists of special bodies of armed men having prisons, etc., at their command.

We are justified in speaking of special bodies of armed men, because the public power which is an attribute of every state 'does not directly coincide' with the armed population, with its 'self-acting armed organization'.

Like all great revolutionary thinkers, Engels tries to draw the attention of the class-conscious workers to what prevailing philistinism regards as least worthy of attention, as the most habitual thing, hallowed by prejudices that are not only deep-rooted but, one might say, petrified. A standing army and police are the chief instruments of state power. But how can it be otherwise?

From the viewpoint of the vast majority of Europeans at the end of the nineteenth century, whom Engels was addressing, and who had not gone through or closely observed a single great revolution, it could not have been otherwise. They could not understand at all what a 'self-acting armed organization of the population' was. When asked why it became necessary to have special bodies of armed men placed above society and alienating themselves from it (police and a standing army), the West-European and Russian philistines are inclined to utter a few phrases borrowed from Spencer or Mikhailovsky, to refer to the growing complexity of social life, the differentiation of functions, and so on.

Such a reference seems 'scientific', and effectively lulls the ordinary person to sleep by obscuring the important and basic fact, namely, the split of society into irreconcilable antagonistic classes.

Were it not for this split, the 'self-acting armed organization of the population' would differ from the primitive organization of a stick-wielding herd of monkeys, or of primitive men, or of men united in clans, by its complexity, its high technical level, and so on. But such an organization would still be possible.

It is impossible because civilized society is split into antagonistic, and, moreover, irreconcilably antagonistic classes, whose 'self-acting' arming would lead to an armed struggle between them. A state arises, a special power is created, special bodies of armed men, and every revolution, by destroying the state apparatus, shows us the naked class struggle, clearly shows us how the ruling class strives to restore the special bodies of armed men which serve it, and how the oppressed class strives to create a new organization of this kind, capable of serving the exploited instead of the exploiters.

In the above argument, Engels raises theoretically the very same question which every great revolution raises before us in practice, palpably and, what is more, on a scale of mass action, namely, the question of the relationship between 'special' bodies of armed men and the 'self-acting armed organization of the population'. We shall see how this question is specifically illustrated by the experience of the European and Russian revolutions.

But to return to Engels's exposition.

He points out that sometimes – in certain parts of North America, for example – this public power is weak (he has in mind a rare exception in capitalist society, and those parts of North America in its pre-imperialist days where the free colonists predominated), but that, generally speaking, it grows stronger:

> It [the public power] grows stronger, however, in proportion as class antagonisms within the state become more acute, and as adjacent states become larger and more populous. We have only to look at our present-day Europe, where class struggle and rivalry in conquest have tuned up the public power to such a pitch that it threatens to swallow the whole of society and even the state.

This was written not later than the early 1890s, Engels's last preface being dated 16 June 1891. The turn towards imperialism – meaning the complete domination of the trusts, the omnipotence of the big banks, a grand-scale colonial policy, and so forth – was only just beginning in France, and was even weaker in North America and in Germany. Since then, 'rivalry in conquest' has taken a gigantic stride, all the more because by the beginning of the second decade of the twentieth century the world had been completely divided up among these 'rivals in conquest', i.e. among the predatory Great Powers. Since then, military and naval armaments have grown fantastically and the predatory war of 1914–17 for the domination of the world by Britain or Germany, for the division of the spoils, has brought the 'swallowing' of all the forces of society by the rapacious state power close to complete catastrophe.

Engels could, as early as 1891, point to 'rivalry in conquest' as one of the most important distinguishing features of the foreign policy of the Great Powers, while the social-chauvinist scoundrels have ever since 1914, when this rivalry, many times intensified, gave rise to an imperialist war, been covering up the defence of the predatory interests of 'their own' bourgeoisie with phrases about 'defence of the fatherland', 'defence of the republic and the revolution', etc.!

III. The State: An Instrument for the Exploitation of the Oppressed Class

The maintenance of the special public power standing above society requires taxes and state loans.

'Having public power and the right to levy taxes,' Engels writes, 'the officials now stand, as organs of society, above society. The free, voluntary respect that was accorded to the organs of the gentile [clan] constitution does not satisfy them, even if they could gain it.' Special laws are enacted proclaiming the sanctity and immunity of the officials. 'The shabbiest police servant' has more 'authority' than the representative of the clan, but even the head of the military power of a civilized state may well envy the elder of a clan the 'unrestrained respect' of society.

The question of the privileged position of the officials as organs of state power is raised here. The main point indicated is: what is it that places them *above* society? We shall see how this theoretical question was answered in practice by the Paris Commune in 1871 and how it was obscured from a reactionary standpoint by Kautsky in 1912.

'Because the state arose from the need to hold class antagonisms in check, but because it arose, at the same time, in the midst of the conflict of these classes, it is, as a rule, the state of the most powerful, economically dominant class, which, through the medium of the state, becomes also the politically dominant class, and thus acquires new means of holding down and exploiting the oppressed class.' The ancient and feudal states were organs for the exploitation of the slaves and serfs; likewise, 'the modern representative state is an instrument of exploitation of wage-labour by capital. By way of exception, however, periods occur in which the warring classes balance each other so nearly that the state power as ostensible mediator acquires, for the moment, a certain degree of independence of both.' Such were the absolute monarchies of the seventeenth and eighteenth centuries, the Bonapartism of the First and Second Empires in France, and the Bismarck regime in Germany.

Such, we may add, is the Kerensky government in republican Russia since it began to persecute the revolutionary proletariat, at a moment when, owing to the leadership of the petty-bourgeois democrats, the Soviets have *already* become impotent, while the bourgeoisie are not *yet* strong enough simply to disperse them.

In a democratic republic, Engels continues, 'wealth exercises its power indirectly, but all the more surely', first, by means of the 'direct corruption of officials' (America); secondly, by means of an 'alliance of the government and the Stock Exchange' (France and America).

At present, imperialism and the domination of the banks have 'developed' into an exceptional art both these methods of upholding and giving effect to the omnipotence of wealth in democratic republics of all descriptions. Since, for instance, in the very first months of the Russian democratic republic, one might say during the honeymoon of the 'socialist' SRs and Mensheviks joined in wedlock to the bourgeoisie, in the coalition government. Mr Palchinsky obstructed every measure intended for curbing the capitalists and their marauding practices, their plundering of the state by means of war contracts; and since later on Mr Palchinsky, upon resigning from the Cabinet (and being, of course, replaced by another quite similar Palchinsky), was 'rewarded' by the capitalists with a lucrative job with a salary of 120,000 roubles per annum – what would you call that?[4] Direct or indirect bribery? An alliance of the government and the syndicates, or 'merely' friendly relations? What role do the Chernovs, Tseretelis, Avksentyevs and Skobelevs play?[5] Are they the 'direct' or only the indirect allies of the millionaire treasury-looters?

Another reason why the omnipotence of 'wealth' is more *certain* in a democratic republic is that it does not depend on defects in the political machinery or on the faulty political shell of capitalism. A democratic republic is the best-possible political shell for capitalism, and, therefore, once capital has gained possession of this very best shell (through the Palchinskys, Chernovs, Tseretelis and co.), it establishes its power so securely, so firmly, that *no* change of persons, institutions or parties in the bourgeois-democratic republic can shake it.

We must also note that Engels is most explicit in calling universal suffrage as well an instrument of bourgeois rule. Universal suffrage, he says, obviously taking account of the long experience of German Social Democracy, is

the gauge of the maturity of the working class. It cannot and never will be anything more in the present-day state.

The petty-bourgeois democrats, such as our Socialist-Revolutionaries and Mensheviks, and also their twin brothers, all the social-chauvinists and opportunists of Western Europe, expect just this 'more' from universal suffrage. They themselves share, and instil into the minds of the people, the false notion that universal suffrage 'in the *present-day* state' is really capable of revealing the will of the majority of the working people and of securing its realization.

Here, we can only indicate this false notion, only point out that Engels's perfectly clear statement is distorted at every step in the propaganda and agitation of the 'official' (i.e. opportunist) socialist parties. A detailed exposure of the utter falsity of this notion which Engels brushes aside here is given in our further account of the views of Marx and Engels on the '*present-day*' state.

Engels gives a general summary of his views in the most popular of his works in the following words:

The state, then, has not existed from all eternity. There have been societies that did without it, that had no idea of the state and state power. At a certain stage of economic development, which was necessarily bound up with the split of society into classes, the state became a necessity owing to this split. We are now rapidly approaching a stage in the development of production at which the existence of these classes not only will have ceased to be a necessity, but will become a positive hindrance to production. They will fall as they arose at an earlier stage. Along with them the state will inevitably fall. Society, which will reorganize production on the basis of a free and equal association of the producers, will put the whole machinery of state where it will then belong: into a museum of antiquities, by the side of the spinning-wheel and the bronze axe.

We do not often come across this passage in the propaganda and agitation literature of the present-day Social Democrats. Even when we do come across it, it is mostly quoted in the same manner as one bows before an icon, i.e. it is done to show official respect for Engels, and no attempt is made to gauge the breadth and depth of the revolution that this relegating of 'the whole machinery of state to a museum of antiquities' implies. In most cases we do not even find an understanding of what Engels calls the state machine.

IV. The 'Withering Away' of the State, and Violent Revolution

Engels's words regarding the 'withering away' of the state are so widely known, they are often quoted, and so clearly reveal the essence of the customary adaptation of Marxism to opportunism that we must deal with them in detail. We shall quote the whole argument from which they are taken.

The proletariat seizes from state power and turns the means of production into state property to begin with. But thereby it abolishes itself as the proletariat, abolishes all class distinctions and class antagonisms, and abolishes also the state as state. Society thus far, operating amid class antagonisms, needed the state, that is, an organization of the particular exploiting class, for the maintenance of its external conditions of production, and, therefore, especially, for the purpose of forcibly keeping the exploited class in the conditions of oppression determined by the given mode of production (slavery, serfdom or bondage, wage-labour). The state was the official representative of society as a whole, its concentration in a visible corporation. But it was this only insofar as it was the state of that class which itself represented, for its own time, society as a whole: in ancient times, the state of slave-owning citizens; in the Middle Ages, of the feudal nobility; in our own time, of the bourgeoisie. When at last it becomes the real representative of the whole of society, it renders itself unnecessary. As soon as there is no longer any social class to be held in subjection, as soon as class rule, and the individual struggle for existence based upon the present anarchy in production, with the collisions and excesses arising from this struggle, are removed, nothing more remains to be held in subjection – nothing necessitating a special coercive force, a state. The first act by which the state really comes forward as the representative of the whole of society – the taking possession of the means of production in the name of society – is also its last independent act as a state. State interference in social relations becomes, in one domain after another, superfluous, and then dies down of itself. The government of persons is replaced by the administration of things, and by the conduct of processes of production. The state is not 'abolished'. *It withers away.* This gives the measure of the value of the phrase 'a free people's state', both as to its justifiable use for a long time from an agitational point of view, and as to its ultimate scientific insufficiency; and also of the so-called anarchists' demand that the state be abolished overnight.

(*Herr Eugen Dühring's Revolution in Science*
[*Anti-Dühring*], third German edition, pp. 301–3)[6]

It is safe to say that of this argument of Engels, which is so remarkably rich in ideas, only one point has become an integral part of socialist thought among modern socialist parties, namely, that according to Marx the state 'withers away' – as distinct from the anarchist doctrine of the 'abolition' of the state. To prune Marxism to such an extent means reducing it to opportunism, for this 'interpretation' only leaves a vague notion of a slow, even, gradual change, of absence of leaps and storms, of absence of revolution. The current, widespread, popular, if one may say so, conception of the 'withering away' of the state undoubtedly means obscuring, if not repudiating, revolution.

Such an 'interpretation', however, is the crudest distortion of Marxism, advantageous only to the bourgeoisie. In point of theory, it is based on disregard for the most important circumstances and considerations indicated in, say, Engels's 'summary' argument we have just quoted in full.

In the first place, at the very outset of his argument, Engels says that, in seizing state power, the proletariat thereby 'abolishes the state as state'. It is not done to ponder over the meaning of this. Generally, it is either ignored altogether, or is considered to be something in the nature of 'Hegelian weakness' on Engels's part. As a matter of fact, however, these words briefly express the experience of one of the greatest proletarian revolutions, the Paris Commune of 1871, of which we shall speak in greater detail in its proper place. As a matter of fact, Engels speaks here of the proletariat revolution 'abolishing' the *bourgeois* state, while the words about the state withering away refer to the remnants of the *proletarian* state *after* the socialist revolution. According to Engels, the bourgeois state does not 'wither away', but is 'abolished' by the proletariat in the course of the revolution. What withers away after this revolution is the proletarian state or semi-state.

Second, the state is a 'special coercive force'. Engels gives this splendid and extremely profound definition here with the utmost lucidity. And from it follows that the 'special coercive force' for the suppression of the proletariat by the bourgeoisie, of millions of working people by handfuls of the rich, must be replaced by a 'special coercive force' for the suppression of the bourgeoisie by the proletariat (the dictatorship of the proletariat). This is precisely what is meant by 'abolition of the state as state'. This is precisely the 'act' of taking possession of the means of production in the name of society. And it is self-evident that *such* a replacement of one (bourgeois) 'special force' by another (proletarian) 'special force' cannot possibly take place in the form of 'withering away'.

Third, in speaking of the state 'withering away', and the even more graphic and colourful 'dying down of itself', Engels refers quite clearly and definitely to the period *after* 'the state has taken possession of the means of production in the name of the whole of society', that is, *after* the socialist revolution. We all know that the political form of the 'state' at that time is the most complete democracy. But it never enters the head of any of the opportunists, who shamelessly distort Marxism, that Engels is consequently speaking here of *democracy* 'dying down of itself', or 'withering away'. This seems very strange at first sight. But it is 'incomprehensible' only to those who have not thought about democracy *also* being a state and, consequently, also disappearing when the state disappears. Revolution alone can 'abolish' the bourgeois state. The state in general, i.e. the most complete democracy, can only 'wither away'.

Fourth, after formulating his famous proposition that 'the state withers away', Engels at once explains specifically that this proposition is directed against both the opportunists and the anarchists. In doing this, Engels puts in the forefront that conclusion, drawn from the proposition that 'the state withers away', which is directed against the opportunists.

One can wager that out of every 10,000 persons who have read or heard about the 'withering away' of the state, 9,990 are completely unaware, or do not remember, that Engels directed his conclusions from that proposition not against anarchists *alone*. And of the remaining ten probably nine do not know the meaning of a 'free people's state' or why an attack on this slogan means an attack on opportunists. This is how history is written! This is how a great revolutionary teaching is imperceptibly falsified and adapted to prevailing philistinism. The conclusion directed against the anarchists has been repeated thousands of times; it has been vulgarized, and rammed into people's heads in the shallowest form, and has acquired the strength of a prejudice, whereas the conclusion directed against the opportunists has been obscured and 'forgotten'!

The 'free people's state' was a programme demand and a catchword current among the German Social Democrats in the 1870s. This catchword is devoid of all political content except that it describes the concept of democracy in a pompous philistine fashion. Insofar as it hinted in a legally permissible manner at a democratic republic, Engels was prepared to 'justify' its use 'for a time' from an agitational point of view. But it was an opportunist catchword, for it amounted to nothing more than prettifying bourgeois democracy, and was also a failure to understand the socialist criticism of the state in general. We are in favour of a democratic republic as the best form of state for the proletariat under capitalism. But we have no right to forget that wage slavery is the lot of the people even in the most democratic bourgeois republic. Furthermore, every state is a 'special force' for the suppression of the oppressed class. Consequently, *every* state is *not* 'free' and *not* a 'people's state'. Marx and Engels explained this repeatedly to their party comrades in the 1870s.

Fifth, the same work of Engels's, whose arguments about the withering away of the state everyone remembers, also contains an argument of the significance of violent revolution. Engels's historical analysis of its role becomes a veritable panegyric on violent revolution. This, 'no one remembers'. It is not done in modern socialist parties to talk or even think about the significance of this idea, and it plays no part whatever in their daily propaganda and agitation among the people. And yet it is inseparably bound up with the 'withering away' of the state into one harmonious whole.

Here is Engels's argument:

That force, however, plays yet another role [other than that of a diabolical power] in history, a revolutionary role; that, in the words of Marx, it is the midwife of every old society which is pregnant with a new one, that it is the instrument with which social movement forces its way through and shatters the dead, fossilized political forms – of this there is not a word in Herr Duhring. It is only with sighs and groans that he admits the possibility that force will perhaps be necessary for the overthrow of an economy based on exploitation – unfortunately, because all use of force demoralizes, he says, the person who uses it. And this in Germany, where a violent collision – which may, after all, be forced on the people – would at least have the advantage of wiping out the servility which has penetrated the nation's mentality following the humiliation of the Thirty Years' War. And this person's mode of thought – dull, insipid, and impotent – presumes to impose itself on the most revolutionary party that history has ever known!

(third German edition, Part II, end of Ch. IV, p. 193)

How can this panegyric on violent revolution, which Engels insistently brought to the attention of the German Social Democrats between 1878 and 1894, i.e. right up to the time of his death, be combined with the theory of the 'withering away' of the state to form a single theory?

Usually, the two are combined by means of eclecticism, by an unprincipled or sophistic selection made arbitrarily (or to please the powers that be) of first one, then another argument, and in ninety-nine cases out of one hundred, if not more, it is the idea of the 'withering away' that is placed in the forefront. Dialectics are replaced by eclecticism – this is the most usual, the most widespread practice to be met with in present-day official Social-Democratic literature in relation to Marxism. This sort of substitution is, of course, nothing new; it was observed even in the history of classical Greek philosophy. In falsifying Marxism in opportunist fashion, the substitution of eclecticism for dialectics is the easiest way of deceiving the people. It gives an illusory satisfaction; it seems to take into account all sides of the process, all trends of development, all the conflicting influences, and so forth, whereas in reality it provides no integral and revolutionary conception of the process of social development at all.

We have already said above, and shall show more fully later, that the theory of Marx and Engels of the inevitability of a violent revolution refers to the bourgeois state. The latter *cannot* be superseded by the proletarian state (the dictatorship of the proletariat) through the process of 'withering away', but, as a general rule, only through a violent revolution. The panegyric Engels sang in its honour, and which fully corresponds to Marx's repeated statements (see the concluding passages of *The Poverty of Philosophy*,[7] and the *Communist Manifesto*,[8] with their proud and open proclamation of the inevitability of a violent revolution; see what Marx wrote nearly thirty years later, in criticizing the Gotha Programme of 1875,[9] when he mercilessly castigated the opportunist character of that programme) – this panegyric is by no means a mere 'impulse', a mere declamation or a polemical sally. The necessity of systematically imbuing the masses with this and precisely this view of violent revolution lies at the root of the entire theory of Marx and Engels. The betrayal of their theory by the now prevailing social-chauvinist and Kautskyite trends expresses itself strikingly in both these trends ignoring *such* propaganda and agitation.

The supersession of the bourgeois state by the proletarian state is impossible without a violent revolution. The abolition of the proletarian state, i.e. of the state in general, is impossible except through the process of 'withering away'.

A detailed and concrete elaboration of these views was given by Marx and Engels when they studied each particular revolutionary situation, when they analysed the lessons of the experience of each particular revolution. We shall now pass to this, undoubtedly the most important, part of their theory.

2

THE EXPERIENCE OF 1848–51

I. The Eve of Revolution

The first works of mature Marxism – *The Poverty of Philosophy* and the *Communist Manifesto* – appeared just on the eve of the revolution of 1848. For this reason, in addition to presenting the general principles of Marxism, they reflect to a certain degree the concrete revolutionary situation of the time. It will, therefore, be more expedient, perhaps, to examine what the authors of these works said about the state immediately before they drew conclusions from the experience of the years 1848–51.

In *The Poverty of Philosophy*, Marx wrote:

The working class, in the course of development, will substitute for the old bourgeois society an association which will preclude classes and their antagonism, and there will be no more political power groups, since the political power is

precisely the official expression of class antagonism in bourgeois society.

(German edition, 1885, p. 182)[1]

It is instructive to compare this general exposition of the idea
of the state disappearing after the abolition of classes with the
exposition contained in the *Communist Manifesto*, written by
Marx and Engels a few months later – in November 1847, to
be exact:

In depicting the most general phases of the development of the
proletariat, we traced the more or less veiled civil war, raging
within existing society up to the point where that war breaks
out into open revolution, and where the violent overthrow of
the bourgeoisie lays the foundation for the sway of the
proletariat . . .

We have seen above that the first step in the revolution by
the working class is to raise the proletariat to the position of the
ruling class to win the battle of democracy.

The proletariat will use its political supremacy to wrest, by
degree, all capital from the bourgeoisie, to centralize all instruments of production in the hands of the state, i.e. of the proletariat organized as the ruling class; and to increase the total
productive forces as rapidly as possible.

(seventh German edition, 1906, pp. 31 and 37)[2]

Here we have a formulation of one of the most remarkable
and most important ideas of Marxism on the subject of the

state, namely, the idea of the 'dictatorship of the proletariat' (as Marx and Engels began to call it after the Paris Commune); and, also, a highly interesting definition of the state, which is also one of the 'forgotten words' of Marxism: *'the state, i.e. the proletariat organized as the ruling class'.*

This definition of the state has never been explained in the prevailing propaganda and agitation literature of the official Social-Democratic parties. More than that, it has been deliberately ignored, for it is absolutely irreconcilable with reformism, and is a slap in the face for the common opportunist prejudices and philistine illusions about the 'peaceful development of democracy'.

The proletariat needs the state – this is repeated by all the opportunists, social-chauvinists and Kautskyites, who assure us that this is what Marx taught. But they 'forget' to add that, in the first place, according to Marx, the proletariat needs only a state which is withering away, i.e. a state so constituted that it begins to wither away immediately, and cannot but wither away. And, second, the working people need a 'state, i.e. the proletariat organized as the ruling class'.

The state is a special organization of force: it is an organization of violence for the suppression of some class. What class must the proletariat suppress? Naturally, only the exploiting class, i.e. the bourgeoisie. The working people need the state only to suppress the resistance of the exploiters, and only the proletariat can direct this suppression, can carry it out. For the proletariat is the only class that is consistently revolutionary, the only class that can unite all the working and exploited people in the struggle against the bourgeoisie, in completely removing it.

The exploiting classes need political rule to maintain exploitation, i.e. in the selfish interests of an insignificant minority against the vast majority of all people. The exploited classes need political rule in order to completely abolish all exploitation, i.e. in the interests of the vast majority of the people, and against the insignificant minority consisting of the modern slave-owners – the landowners and capitalists.

The petty-bourgeois democrats, those sham socialists who replaced the class struggle by dreams of class harmony, even pictured the socialist transformation in a dreamy fashion – not as the overthrow of the rule of the exploiting class, but as the peaceful submission of the minority to the majority which has become aware of its aims. This petty-bourgeois utopia, which is inseparable from the idea of the state being above classes, led in practice to the betrayal of the interests of the working classes, as was shown, for example, by the history of the French revolutions of 1848 and 1871, and by the experience of 'socialist' participation in bourgeois cabinets in Britain, France, Italy and other countries at the turn of the century.

All his life Marx fought against this petty-bourgeois socialism, now revived in Russia by the Socialist-Revolutionary and Menshevik parties. He developed his theory of the class struggle consistently, down to the theory of political power, of the state.

The overthrow of bourgeois rule can be accomplished only by the proletariat, the particular class whose economic conditions of existence prepare it for this task and provide it with the possibility and the power to perform it. While the bourgeoisie break up and disintegrate the peasantry and all the petty-bourgeois groups, they weld together, unite and organize the proletariat. Only the proletariat – by virtue of the economic role it plays in large-scale production – is capable of being the leader of *all* the working and exploited people, whom the bourgeoisie exploit, oppress and crush, often not less but more than they do the proletarians, but who are incapable of waging an *independent* struggle for their emancipation.

The theory of class struggle, applied by Marx to the question of the state and the socialist revolution, leads as a matter of course to the recognition of the *political rule* of the proletariat, of its dictatorship, i.e. of undivided power directly backed by the armed force of the people. The overthrow of the bourgeoisie can be achieved only by the proletariat becoming the *ruling class*, capable of crushing the inevitable and desperate resistance of the bourgeoisie, and of organizing *all* the working and exploited people for the new economic system.

The proletariat needs state power, a centralized organization of force, an organization of violence, both to crush the resistance of the exploiters and to *lead* the enormous mass of the population – the peasants, the petty bourgeoisie, and semi-proletarians – in the work of organizing a socialist economy.

By educating the workers' party, Marxism educates the vanguard of the proletariat, capable of assuming power and *leading the whole people* to socialism, of directing and organizing the new system, of being the teacher, the guide, the leader of all the working and exploited people in organizing their social life without the bourgeoisie and against the bourgeoisie. By contrast, the opportunism now prevailing trains the members of the workers' party to be the representatives of the better-paid workers, who lose touch with the masses, 'get along' fairly well under capitalism, and sell their birthright for a mass of pottage, i.e. renounce their role as revolutionary leaders of the people against the bourgeoisie.

Marx's theory of 'the state, i.e. the proletariat organized as the ruling class', is inseparably bound up with the whole of his doctrine of the revolutionary role of the proletariat in history. The culmination of this rule is the proletarian dictatorship, the political rule of the proletariat.

But since the proletariat needs the state as a *special* form of organization of violence *against* the bourgeoisie, the following conclusion suggests itself: is it conceivable that such an organization can be created without first abolishing, destroying the state machine created by the bourgeoisie *for themselves*? The *Communist Manifesto* leads straight to this conclusion, and it is of this conclusion that Marx speaks when summing up the experience of the revolution of 1848–51.

II. The Revolution Summed Up

Marx sums up his conclusions from the revolution of 1848–51, on the subject of the state we are concerned with, in the following argument contained in *The Eighteenth Brumaire of Louis Bonaparte*:

> But the revolution is throughgoing. It is still journeying through purgatory. It does its work methodically. By 2 December 1851 [the day of Louis Bonaparte's *coup d'état*], it had completed one half of its preparatory work. It is now completing the other half. First it perfected the parliamentary power, in order to be able to overthrow it. Now that it has attained this, it is perfecting the executive power, reducing it to its purest expression, isolating it, setting it up against itself as the sole object, in order to concentrate all its forces of destruction against it. And when it has done this second half of its preliminary work, Europe will leap from its seat and exultantly exclaim: well grubbed, old mole! . . .
>
> This executive power with its enormous bureaucratic and military organization, with its vast and ingenious state machinery, with a host of officials numbering half a million, besides an army of another half million, this appalling parasitic body, which enmeshes the body of French society and chokes all its pores, sprang up in the days of the absolute

monarchy, with the decay of the feudal system, which it helped to hasten.

The first French Revolution developed centralization, 'but at the same time' it increased 'the extent, the attributes and the number of agents of governmental power. Napoleon completed this state machinery.' The legitimate monarchy and the July monarchy 'added nothing but a greater division of labour'.

> Finally, in its struggle against the revolution, the parliamentary republic found itself compelled to strengthen, along with repressive measures, the resources and centralization of governmental power. All revolutions perfected this machine instead of smashing it. The parties that contended in turn for domination regarded the possession of this huge state edifice as the principal spoils of the victor.
>
> (*The Eighteenth Brumaire of Louis Bonaparte*, fourth edition, Hamburg, 1907, pp. 98–9)[3]

In this remarkable argument, Marxism takes a tremendous step forward compared with the *Communist Manifesto*. In the latter, the question of the state is still treated in an extremely abstract manner, in the most general terms and expressions. In the above-quoted passage, the question is treated in a concrete manner, and the conclusion is extremely precise, definite, practical and palpable: all previous revolutions perfected the state machine, whereas it must be broken, smashed.

This conclusion is the chief and fundamental point in the Marxist theory of the state. And it is precisely this fundamental point which has been completely *ignored* by the dominant official Social-Democratic parties and, indeed, *distorted* (as we shall see later) by the foremost theoretician of the Second International, Karl Kautsky.

The *Communist Manifesto* gives a general summary of history, which compels us to regard the state as the organ of class rule and leads us to the inevitable conclusion that the proletariat cannot overthrow the bourgeoisie without first winning political power, without attaining political supremacy, without transforming the state into the 'proletariat organized as the ruling class'; and that this proletarian state will begin to wither away immediately after its victory because the state is unnecessary and cannot exist in a society in which there are no class antagonisms. The question as to how, from the point of view of historical development, the replacement of the bourgeois by the proletarian state is to take place is not raised here.

This is the question Marx raises and answers in 1852. True to his philosophy of dialectical materialism, Marx takes as his basis the historical experience of the great years of revolution, 1848 to 1851. Here, as everywhere else, his theory is a *summing up* of experience, illuminated by a profound philosophical conception of the world and a rich knowledge of history.

The problem of the state is put specifically: How did the bourgeois state, the state machine necessary for the rule of the bourgeoisie, come into being historically? What changes did it undergo, what evolution did it perform in the course of bourgeois revolutions and in the face of the independent actions of the oppressed classes? What are the tasks of the proletariat in relation to this state machine?

The centralized state power that is peculiar to bourgeois society came into being in the period of the fall of absolutism. Two institutions most characteristic of this state machine are the bureaucracy and the standing army. In their works, Marx and Engels repeatedly show that the bourgeoisie are connected with these institutions by thousands of threads. Every worker's experience illustrates this connection in an extremely graphic and impressive manner. From its own bitter experience, the working class learns to recognize this connection. That is why it so easily grasps and so firmly learns the doctrine which shows the inevitability of this connection, a doctrine which the petty-bourgeois democrats either ignorantly and flippantly deny, or still more flippantly admit 'in general', while forgetting to draw appropriate practical conclusions.

The bureaucracy and the standing army are a 'parasite' on the body of bourgeois society – a parasite created by the internal antagonisms which rend that society, but a parasite which 'chokes' all its vital pores. The Kautskyite opportunism now prevailing in official Social Democracy considers the view that the state is a *parasitic organism* to be the peculiar and exclusive attribute of anarchism. It goes without saying that this distortion of Marxism is of vast advantage to those philistines who have reduced socialism to the unheard-of disgrace of justifying and prettifying the imperialist war by applying to it the concept of 'defence of the fatherland'; but it is unquestionably a distortion, nevertheless.

The development, perfection, and strengthening of the bureaucratic and military apparatus proceeded during all the numerous bourgeois revolutions which Europe has witnessed since the fall of feudalism. In particular, it is the petty bourgeois who are attracted to the side of the big bourgeoisie and are largely subordinated to them through this apparatus, which provides the upper sections of the peasants, small artisans, tradesmen, and the like with comparatively comfortable, quiet, and respectable jobs raising the holders *above* the people. Consider what happened in Russia during the six months following 27 February 1917. The official posts which formerly were given by preference to the Black Hundreds have now become the spoils of the Cadets,[4] Mensheviks, and Socialist-Revolutionaries. Nobody has really thought of introducing any serious reforms. Every effort has been made to put them off 'until the Constituent Assembly meets', and to steadily put off its convocation until after the war! But there has been no delay, no waiting for the Constituent Assembly, in the matter of dividing the spoils of getting the lucrative jobs of ministers, deputy ministers, governors-general, etc., etc.! The game of combinations that has been played in forming the government has been, in essence, only an expression of this division and redivision of the 'spoils', which has been going on above and below, throughout the country, in every department of central and local government. The six months between 27 February and 27 August 1917 can be summed up, objectively summed up beyond all dispute, as follows: reforms shelved, distribution of official jobs accomplished and 'mistakes' in the distribution corrected by a few redistributions.

But the more the bureaucratic apparatus is 'redistributed' among the various bourgeois and petty-bourgeois parties (among the Cadets, Socialist-Revolutionaries and Mensheviks in the case of Russia), the more keenly aware the oppressed classes, and the proletariat at their head, become of their irreconcilable hostility to the *whole* of bourgeois society. Hence the need for all bourgeois parties, even for the most democratic and 'revolutionary-democratic' among them, to intensify repressive measures against the revolutionary proletariat, to strengthen the apparatus of coercion, i.e. the state machine. This course of events compels the revolution '*to concentrate all its forces of destruction*' against the state power, and to set itself the aim, not of improving the state machine, but of *smashing and destroying* it.

It was not logical reasoning, but actual developments, the actual experience of 1848–51, that led to the matter being presented in this way. The extent to which Marx held strictly to the solid ground of historical experience can be seen from the fact that, in 1852, he did not yet specifically raise the question of *what* was to take the place of the state machine to be destroyed. Experience had not yet provided material for dealing with this question, which history placed on the agenda later on, in 1871. In 1852, all that could be established with the accuracy of scientific observation was that the proletarian revolution *had approached* the task of 'concentrating all its forces of destruction' against the state power, of 'smashing' the state machine.

Here the question may arise: is it correct to generalize the experience, observations and conclusions of Marx, to apply them to a field that is wider than the history of France during the three years 1848–51? Before proceeding to deal with this question, let us recall a remark made by Engels and then examine the facts. In his introduction to the third edition of *The Eighteenth Brumaire*, Engels wrote:

> France is the country where, more than anywhere else, the historical class struggles were each time fought out to a finish, and where, consequently, the changing political forms within which they move and in which their results are summarized have been stamped in the sharpest outlines. The centre of feudalism in the Middle Ages, the model country, since the Renaissance, of a unified monarchy based on social estates, France demolished feudalism in the Great Revolution and established the rule of the bourgeoisie in a classical purity unequalled by any other European land. And the struggle of the upward-striving proletariat against the ruling bourgeoisie appeared here in an acute form unknown elsewhere.
>
> (1907 edition, p. 4)

The last remark is out of date insomuch as since 1871 there has been a lull in the revolutionary struggle of the French proletariat, although, long as this lull may be, it does not at all preclude the possibility that in the coming proletarian revolution France may show herself to be the classic country of the class struggle to a finish.

Let us, however, cast a general glance over the history of the advanced countries at the turn of the century. We shall see that the same process went on more slowly, in more varied forms, in a much wider field: on the one hand, the development of 'parliamentary power' both in the republican countries (France, America, Switzerland), and in the monarchies (Britain, Germany to a certain extent, Italy, the Scandinavia countries, etc.); on the other hand, a struggle for power among the various bourgeois and petty-bourgeois parties which distributed and redistributed the 'spoils' of office, with the foundations of bourgeois society unchanged; and, lastly, the perfection and consolidation of the 'executive power', of its bureaucratic and military apparatus.

There is not the slightest doubt that these features are common to the whole of the modern evolution of all capitalist states in general. In the last three years 1848–51 France displayed, in a swift, sharp, concentrated form, the very same processes of development which are peculiar to the whole capitalist world.

Imperialism – the era of bank capital, the era of gigantic capitalist monopolies, of the development of monopoly capitalism into state-monopoly capitalism – has clearly shown an unprecedented growth in its bureaucratic and military apparatus in connection with the intensification of repressive measures against the proletariat both in the monarchical and in the freest, republican countries.

World history is now undoubtedly leading, on an incomparably larger scale than in 1852, to the 'concentration of all the forces' of the proletarian revolution on the 'destruction' of the state machine.

What the proletariat will put in its place is suggested by the highly instructive material furnished by the Paris Commune.

III. The Presentation of the Question by Marx in 1852

In 1907, Mehring,[5] in the magazine *Neue Zeit*, (Vol. XXV, 2, p. 164),[6] published extracts from Marx's letter to Weydemeyer[7] dated 5 March 1852. This letter, among other things, contains the following remarkable observation:

And now as to myself, no credit is due to me for discovering the existence of classes in modern society or the struggle between them. Long before me bourgeois historians had described the historical development of this class struggle and bourgeois economists, the economic anatomy of classes. What I did that was new was to prove: (1) that the existence of classes is only bound up with the particular, historical phases in the development of production (*historische Entwicklungsphasen der Produktion*), (2) that the class struggle necessarily leads to the dictatorship of the proletariat, (3) that this dictatorship itself only constitutes the transition to the abolition of all classes and to a classless society.[8]

In these words, Marx succeeded in expressing with striking clarity, first, the chief and radical difference between his theory and that of the foremost and most profound thinkers of the bourgeoisie; and, second, the essence of his theory of the state.

It is often said and written that the main point in Marx's theory is the class struggle. But this is wrong. And this wrong notion very often results in an opportunist distortion of Marxism and its falsification in a spirit acceptable to the bourgeoisie. For the theory of the class struggle was created *not* by Marx *but* by the bourgeoisie *before* Marx, and, generally speaking, it is *acceptable* to the bourgeoisie. Those who recognize *only* the class struggle are not yet Marxists; they may be found to be still within the bounds of bourgeois thinking and bourgeois politics. To confine Marxism to the theory of the class struggle means curtailing Marxism, distorting it, reducing it to something acceptable to the bourgeoisie. Only he is a Marxist who *extends* the recognition of the class struggle to the recognition of the *dictatorship of the proletariat*. That is what constitutes the most profound distinction between the Marxist and the ordinary petty (as well as big) bourgeois. This is the touchstone on which the *real* understanding and recognition of Marxism should be tested. And it is not surprising that when the

history of Europe brought the working class face to face
with this question as a *practical* issue, not only all the opportunists and reformists, but all the Kautskyites (people who
vacillate between reformism and Marxism) proved to be
miserable philistines and petty-bourgeois democrats *repudiating* the dictatorship of the proletariat. Kautsky's pamphlet,
The Dictatorship of the Proletariat, published in August 1918,
i.e. long after the first edition of the present book, is a
perfect example of petty-bourgeois distortion of Marxism
and base renunciation of it in deeds, while hypocritically
recognizing it *in words* (see my pamphlet, *The Proletarian
Revolution and the Renegade Kautsky*, Petrograd and
Moscow, 1918).

Opportunism today, as represented by its principal
spokesman, the ex-Marxist Karl Kautsky, fits in completely
with Marx's characterization of the bourgeois position
quoted above, for this opportunism limits recognition of the
class struggle to the sphere of bourgeois relations. (Within
this sphere, within its framework, not a single educated
liberal will refuse to recognize the class struggle 'in principle'!) Opportunism *does not extend* recognition of the class
struggle to the cardinal point, to the period of *transition*
from capitalism to communism, of the *overthrow* and the
complete *abolition* of the bourgeoisie. In reality, this period
inevitably is a period of an unprecedentedly violent class
struggle in unprecedentedly acute forms, and, consequently,
during this period the state must inevitably be a state that is
democratic *in a new way* (for the proletariat and the

propertyless in general) and dictatorial *in a new way* (against the bourgeoisie).

Further. The essence of Marx's theory of the state has been mastered only by those who realize that the dictatorship of a *single* class is necessary not only for every class society in general, not only for the *proletariat* which has overthrown the bourgeoisie, but also for the entire *historical period* which separates capitalism from 'classless society', from communism. Bourgeois states are most varied in form, but their essence is the same: all these states, whatever their form, in the final analysis are inevitably the *dictatorship of the bourgeoisie*. The transition from capitalism to communism is certainly bound to yield a tremendous abundance and variety of political forms, but the essence will inevitably be the same: *the dictatorship of the proletariat*.

3

EXPERIENCE OF THE PARIS COMMUNE OF 1871: MARX'S ANALYSIS

I. What Made the Communards' Attempt Heroic?

It is well known that in the autumn of 1870, a few months before the Commune, Marx warned the Paris workers that any attempt to overthrow the government would be the folly of despair. But when, in March 1871, a decisive battle was forced upon the workers and they accepted it – when the uprising had become a fact – Marx greeted the proletarian revolution with the greatest enthusiasm, in spite of unfavourable auguries. Marx did not persist in the pedantic attitude of condemning an 'untimely' movement as did the ill-famed Russian renegade from Marxism, Plekhanov, who in November 1905 wrote encouragingly about the workers' and peasants' struggle, but after December 1905 cried, liberal fashion: 'They should not have taken up arms.'

Marx, however, was not only enthusiastic about the heroism of the Communards, who, as he expressed it, 'stormed heaven'. Although the mass revolutionary movement did not achieve its aim, he regarded it as a historic experience of enormous importance, as a certain advance of the world proletarian revolution, as a practical step that was more important than hundreds of programmes and arguments. Marx endeavoured to analyse this experiment, to draw tactical lessons from it and re-examine his theory in the light of it.

The only 'correction' Marx thought it necessary to make to the *Communist Manifesto* he made on the basis of the revolutionary experience of the Paris Commune.

The last preface to the new German edition of the *Communist Manifesto*, signed by both its authors, is dated 24 June 1872. In this preface the authors, Karl Marx and Frederick Engels say that the programme of the *Communist Manifesto* 'has in some details become out-of-date', and they go on to say:

> One thing especially was proved by the Commune, viz., that 'the working class cannot simply lay hold of the ready-made state machinery and wield it for its own purposes'[1]

The authors took the words that are in single quotation marks in this passage from Marx's book, *The Civil War in France*.

Thus, Marx and Engels regarded one principal and fundamental lesson of the Paris Commune as being of such enormous importance that they introduced it as an important correction into the *Communist Manifesto*.

Most characteristically, it is this important correction that has been distorted by the opportunists, and its meaning probably is not known to nine-tenths, if not ninety-nine-hundredths, of the readers of the *Communist Manifesto*. We shall deal with this distortion more fully farther on, in a chapter devoted specially to distortions. Here it will be sufficient to note that the current, vulgar 'interpretation' of Marx's famous statement just quoted is that Marx here allegedly emphasizes the idea of slow development in contradistinction to the seizure of power, and so on.

As a matter of fact, *the exact opposite is the case*. Marx's idea is that the working class must *break up*, *smash* the 'ready-made state machinery', and not confine itself merely to laying hold of it.

On 12 April 1871, i.e. just at the time of the Commune, Marx wrote to Kugelmann:[2]

> If you look up the last chapter of my *Eighteenth Brumaire*, you will find that I declare that the next attempt of the French Revolution will be no longer, as before, to transfer the bureaucratic-military machine from one hand to another, but to *smash* it [Marx's italics – the original is *zerbrechen*], and this is the precondition for every real people's revolution on the Continent. And this is what our heroic Party comrades in Paris are attempting.
>
> (*Neue Zeit*, Vol. XX, 1, 1901–2, p. 709)[3]

The words, 'to smash the bureaucratic-military machine', briefly express the principal lesson of Marxism regarding the tasks of the proletariat during a revolution in relation to the state. And this is the lesson that has been not only completely ignored but positively distorted by the prevailing, Kautskyite, 'interpretation' of Marxism!

As for Marx's reference to *The Eighteenth Brumaire*, we have quoted the relevant passage in full above.

It is interesting to note, in particular, two points in the above-quoted argument of Marx. First, he restricts his conclusion to the Continent. This was understandable in 1871, when Britain was still the model of a purely capitalist country, but without a militarist clique and, to a considerable degree, without a bureaucracy. Marx therefore excluded Britain, where a revolution, even a people's revolution, then seemed possible, and indeed was possible, *without* the precondition of destroying 'ready-made state machinery'.

Today, in 1917, at the time of the first great imperialist war, this restriction made by Marx is no longer valid. Both Britain and America, the biggest and the last representatives – in the whole world – of Anglo-Saxon 'liberty', in the sense that they had no militarist cliques and bureaucracy, have completely sunk into the all-European filthy, bloody morass of bureaucratic-military institutions which subordinate everything to themselves, and suppress everything. Today, in Britain and America, too, 'the precondition for every real people's revolution' is the *smashing*, the *destruction* of the 'ready-made state machinery' (made and brought up to the 'European', general imperialist, perfection in those countries in the years 1914–17).

Second, particular attention should be paid to Marx's extremely profound remark that the destruction of the bureaucratic-military state machine is 'the precondition for every real *people's* revolution'. This idea of a 'people's' revolution seems strange coming from Marx, so that the Russian Plekhanovites and Mensheviks, those followers of Struve who wish to be regarded as Marxists, might possibly declare such an expression to be a 'slip of the pen' on Marx's part. They have reduced Marxism to such a state of wretchedly liberal distortion that nothing exists for them beyond the antithesis between bourgeois revolution and proletarian revolution, and even this antithesis they interpret in an utterly lifeless way.

If we take the revolutions of the twentieth century as examples we shall, of course, have to admit that the Portuguese and the Turkish revolutions are both bourgeois revolutions. Neither of them, however, is a 'people's' revolution, since in neither does the mass of the people, their vast majority, come out actively, independently, with their own economic and political demands to any noticeable degree. By contrast, although the Russian bourgeois revolution of 1905–7 displayed no such 'brilliant' successes as at times fell to the Portuguese and Turkish revolutions, it was undoubtedly a 'real people's' revolution, since the mass of the people, their majority, the very lowest social groups, crushed by oppression and exploitation, rose independently and stamped on the entire course of the revolution the imprint of *their* own demands, *their* attempt to build in their own way a new society in place of the old society that was being destroyed.

In Europe, in 1871, the proletariat did not constitute the majority of the people in any country on the Continent. A 'people's' revolution, one actually sweeping the majority into its stream, could be such only if it embraced both the proletariat and the peasants. These two classes then constituted the 'people'. These two classes are united by the fact that the 'bureaucratic-military state machine' oppresses, crushes, exploits them. To *smash* this machine, *to break it up*, is truly in the interest of the 'people', of their majority, of the workers and most of the peasants, is 'the precondition' for a free alliance of the poor peasant and the proletarians, whereas without such an alliance democracy is unstable and socialist transformation is impossible.

As is well known, the Paris Commune was actually working its way towards such an alliance, although it did not reach its goal owing to a number of circumstances, internal and external.

Consequently, in speaking of a 'real people's revolution', Marx, without in the least discounting the special features of the petty bourgeois (he spoke a great deal about them and often), took strict account of the actual balance of class forces in most of the continental countries of Europe in 1871. On the other hand, he stated that the 'smashing' of the state machine was required by the interests of both the workers and the peasants, that it united them, that it placed before them the common task of removing the 'parasite' and of replacing it by something new.

By what exactly?

II. What Is to Replace the Smashed State Machine?

In 1847, in the *Communist Manifesto*, Marx's answer to this question was as yet a purely abstract one; to be exact, it was an answer that indicated the tasks, but not the ways of accomplishing them. The answer given in the *Communist Manifesto* was that this machine was to be replaced by 'the proletariat organized as the ruling class', by the 'winning of the battle of democracy'.

Marx did not indulge in utopias; he expected the *experience* of the mass movement to provide the reply to the question as to the specific forms this organization of the proletariat as the ruling class would assume and as to the exact manner in which this organization would be combined with the most complete, most consistent 'winning of the battle of democracy'.

Marx subjected the experience of the Commune, meagre as it was, to the most careful analysis in *The Civil War in France*. Let us quote the most important passages of this work.[4]

Originating from the Middle Ages, there developed in the nineteenth century 'the centralized state power, with its ubiquitous organs of standing army, police, bureaucracy, clergy, and judicature'. With the development of class antagonisms between capital and labour, 'state power assumed more and more the character of a public force organized for the suppression of the working class, of a machine of class rule. After every revolution, which marks an advance in the class struggle, the purely coercive character of the state power stands out in bolder and bolder relief.' After the revolution of 1848–49, state power became 'the national war instruments of capital against labour'. The Second Empire consolidated this.

The direct antithesis to the empire was the Commune. It was the 'specific form' of 'a republic that was not only to remove the monarchical form of class rule, but class rule itself'.

What was this 'specific' form of the proletarian, socialist republic? What was the state it began to create?

> The first decree of the Commune, therefore, was the suppression of the standing army, and the substitution for it of the armed people.

This demand now figures in the programme of every party calling itself socialist. The real worth of their programme, however, is best shown by the behaviour of our Socialist-Revolutionaries and Mensheviks, who, right after the revolution of 27 February, refused to carry out this demand!

> The Commune was formed of the municipal councillors, chosen by universal suffrage in the various wards of the town, responsible and revocable at any time. The majority of its members were naturally working men, or acknowledged representatives of the working class . . . The police, which until then had been the instrument of the Government, was at once

stripped of its political attributes, and turned into the responsible, and at all times revocable, agent of the Commune. So were
the officials of all other branches of the administration. From
the members of the Commune downwards, the public service
had to be done at *workmen's wages*. The privileges and the
representation allowances of the high dignitaries of state disappeared along with the high dignitaries themselves . . . Having
once got rid of the standing army and the police, the instruments of physical force of the old government, the Commune
proceeded at once to break the instrument of spiritual suppression, the power of the priests . . . The judicial functionaries lost
that sham independence . . . they were thenceforward to be
elective, responsible, and revocable.[5]

The Commune, therefore, appears to have replaced the
smashed state machine 'only' by fuller democracy: abolition of the standing army; all officials to be elected
and subject to recall. But, as a matter of fact, this 'only'
signifies a gigantic replacement of certain institutions by
other institutions of a fundamentally different type. This is
exactly a case of 'quantity being transformed into quality':
democracy, introduced as fully and consistently as is at all
conceivable, is transformed from bourgeois into proletarian democracy; from the state (= a special force for the
suppression of a particular class) into something which is
no longer the state proper.

It is still necessary to suppress the bourgeoisie and crush
their resistance. This was particularly necessary for the

Commune; and one of the reasons for its defeat was that it did not do this with sufficient determination. The organ of suppression, however, is here the majority of the population, and not a minority, as was always the case under slavery, serfdom, and wage slavery. And since the majority of people *itself* suppresses its oppressors, a 'special force' for suppression is *no longer necessary*! In this sense, the state *begins to wither away*. Instead of the special institutions of a privileged minority (privileged officialdom, the chiefs of the standing army), the majority itself can directly fulfil all these functions, and the more the functions of state power are performed by the people as a whole, the less need there is for the existence of this power.

In this connection, the following measures of the Commune, emphasized by Marx, are particularly noteworthy: the abolition of all representation allowances, and of all monetary privileges to officials, the reduction of the remuneration of *all* servants of the state to the level of *'workmen's wages'*. This shows more clearly than anything else the turn from bourgeois to proletarian democracy, from the democracy of the oppressors to that of the oppressed classes, from the state as a *'special force'* for the suppression of a particular class to the suppression of the oppressors by the *general force* of the majority of the people – the workers and the peasants. And it is on this particularly striking point, perhaps the most important as far as the problem of the state is concerned, that the ideas of Marx have been most completely ignored! In popular commentaries, the number of which is legion, this is not mentioned. The thing done is to keep silent about it as if it were a piece of old-fashioned '*naïveté*', just as Christians, after their religion had been given the status of state religion, 'forgot' the '*naïveté*' of primitive Christianity with its democratic revolutionary spirit.

The reduction of the remuneration of high state officials seem 'simply' a demand of naïve, primitive democracy. One of the 'founders' of modern opportunism, the ex–Social Democrat Eduard Bernstein,[6] has more than once repeated the vulgar bourgeois jeers at 'primitive' democracy. Like all opportunists, and like the present Kautskyites, he did not understand at all that, first of all, the transition from capitalism to socialism is *impossible* without a certain 'reversion' to 'primitive' democracy (for how else can the majority, and then the whole population without exception, proceed to discharge state functions?); and that, second, 'primitive democracy' based on capitalism and capitalist culture is not the same as primitive democracy in prehistoric or precapitalist times. Capitalist culture has *created* large-scale production, factories, railways, the postal service, telephones, etc., and *on this basis* the great majority of the functions of the old 'state power' have become so simplified and can be reduced to such exceedingly simple operations of registration, filing and checking that they can be easily performed by every literate person, can quite easily be performed for ordinary 'workmen's wages', and that these functions can (and must) be stripped of every shadow of privilege, of every semblance of 'official grandeur'.

All officials, without exception, elected and subject to recall *at any time*, their salaries reduced to the level of ordinary 'workmen's wages' — these simple and 'self-evident' democratic measures, while completely uniting the interests of the workers and the majority of the peasants, at the same time serve as a bridge leading from capitalism to socialism. These measures concern the reorganization of the state, the purely political reorganization of society; but, of course, they acquire their full meaning and significance only in connection with the 'expropriation of the expropriators' either bring accomplished or in preparation, i.e. with the transformation of capitalist private ownership of the means of production into social ownership.

'The Commune,' Marx wrote, 'made the catchword of all bourgeois revolutions, cheap government, a reality, by abolishing the two greatest sources of expenditure — the army and the officialdom.' From the peasants, as from other sections of the petty bourgeoisie, only an insignificant few 'rise to the top', 'get on in the world' in the bourgeois sense, i.e. become either well-to-do, bourgeois, or officials in secure and privileged positions. In every capitalist country where there are peasants (as there are in most capitalist countries), the vast majority of them are oppressed by the government and long for its overthrow, long for 'cheap' government. This can be achieved *only* by the proletariat; and by achieving it, the proletariat at the same time takes a step towards the socialist reorganization of the state.

III. Abolition of Parliamentarism

'The Commune,' Marx wrote, 'was to be a working, not a parliamentary, body, executive and legislative at the same time':

> Instead of deciding once in three or six years which member of the ruling class was to represent and repress [*ver-* and *zertreten*] the people in parliament, universal suffrage was to serve the people constituted in communes, as individual suffrage serves every other employer in the search for workers, foremen and accountants for his business.

Owing to the prevalence of social-chauvinism and opportunism, this remarkable criticism of parliamentarism, made in 1871, also belongs now to the 'forgotten words' of Marxism. The professional cabinet ministers and parliamentarians, the traitors to the proletariat and the 'practical' socialists of our day, have left all criticism of parliamentarism to the anarchists, and, on this wonderfully reasonable ground, they denounce *all* criticism of parliamentarism as 'anarchism'!! It is not surprising that the proletariat of the 'advanced' parliamentary countries, disgusted with such 'socialists' as the Scheidemanns, Davids, Legiens, Sembats, Renaudels, Hendersons, Vanderveldes, Staunings, Brantings, Bissolatis and co., has been with increasing frequency giving its sympathies to anarcho-syndicalism, in spite of the fact that the latter is merely the twin brother of opportunism.[7]

For Marx, however, revolutionary dialectics was never the empty fashionable phrase, the toy rattle, which Plekhanov, Kautsky and others have made of it. Marx knew how to break with anarchism ruthlessly for its inability to make use even of the 'pigsty' of bourgeois parliamentarism, especially when the situation was obviously not revolutionary; but, at the same time, he knew how to subject parliamentarism to genuinely revolutionary proletarian criticism.

To decide once every few years which members of the ruling class is to repress and crush the people through parliament – this is the real essence of bourgeois parliamentarism, not only in parliamentary – constitutional monarchies, but also in the most democratic republics.

But if we deal with the question of the state, and if we consider parliamentarism as one of the institutions of the state, from the point of view of the tasks of the proletariat in *this* field, what is the way out of parliamentarism? How can it be dispensed with?

Once again, we must say: the lessons of Marx, based on the study of the Commune, have been so completely forgotten that the present-day 'Social Democrat' (i.e. present-day traitor to socialism) really cannot understand any criticism of parliamentarism other than anarchist or reactionary criticism.

The way out of parliamentarism is not, of course, the abolition of representative institutions and the elective principle, but the conversion of the representative institutions from talking shops into 'working' bodies. 'The Commune was to be a working, not a parliamentary, body, executive and legislative at the same time.'

'A working, not a parliamentary body' – this is a blow straight from the shoulder at the present-day parliamentarian country, from America to Switzerland, from France to Britain, Norway, and so forth – in these countries the real business of 'state' is performed behind the scenes and is carried on by the departments, chancelleries, and general staffs; parliament is given up to talk for the special purpose of fooling the 'common people'. This is so true that even in the Russian republic, a bourgeois-democratic republic, all these sins of parliamentarism came out at once, even before it managed to set up a real parliament. The heroes of rotten philistinism, such as the Skobelevs and Tseretelis, the Chernovs and Avksentyevs, have even succeeded in polluting the Soviets after the fashion of the most disgusting bourgeois parliamentarism, in converting them into mere talking shops. In the Soviets, the 'socialist' ministers are fooling the credulous rustics with phrase-mongering and resolutions. In the government itself, a sort of permanent shuffle is going on in order that, on the one hand, as many Socialist-Revolutionaries and Mensheviks as possible may in turn get near the 'pie', the lucrative and honourable posts, and that, on the other hand, the 'attention' of the people may be 'engaged'. Meanwhile the chancelleries and army staffs 'do' the business of 'state'.

Dyelo Naroda, the organ of the ruling Socialist-Revolutionary Party, recently admitted in a leading article – with the matchless frankness of people of 'good society', in which 'all' are engaged in political prostitution – that even in the ministries headed by the 'socialists' (please excuse the expression!), the whole bureaucratic apparatus is in fact unchanged, is working in the old way and quite 'freely' sabotaging revolutionary measures! Even without this admission, does not the actual history of the participation of the Socialist-Revolutionaries and Mensheviks in the government prove this? It is noteworthy, however, that in the ministerial company of the Cadets, the Chernovs, Rusanovs, Zenzinovs and other editors of *Dyelo Naroda* have so completely lost all sense of shame as to brazenly assert, as if it were a mere bagatelle, that in 'their' ministries everything is unchanged!![8] Revolutionary-democratic phrases to gull the rural Simple Simons, and bureaucracy and red tape to 'gladden the hearts' of the capitalists – that is the *essence* of the 'honest' coalition.

The Commune substitutes for the venal and rotten parliamentarism of bourgeois society institutions in which freedom of opinion and discussion does not degenerate into deception, for the parliamentarians themselves have to work, have to execute their own laws, have themselves to test the results achieved in reality, and to account directly to their constituents. Representative institutions remain, but there is *no* parliamentarism here as a special system, as the division of labour between the legislative and the executive, as a privileged position for the deputies. We cannot imagine democracy, even proletarian democracy, without representative institutions, but we can and *must* imagine democracy without parliamentarism, if criticism of bourgeois society is not mere

words for us, if the desire to overthrow the rule of the bourgeoisie is our earnest and sincere desire, and not a mere 'election' cry for catching workers' votes, as it is with the
Mensheviks and Socialist-Revolutionaries, and also the
Scheidemanns and Legiens, the Semblats and Vanderveldes.

It is extremely instructive to note that, in speaking of the
function of those officials who are necessary for the Commune
and for proletarian democracy, Marx compares them to the
workers of 'every other employer', that is, of the ordinary capitalist enterprise, with its 'workers, foremen, and accountants'.

There is no trace of utopianism in Marx, in the sense that
he made up or invented a 'new' society. No, he studied the
birth of the new society *out* of the old, and the forms of transition from the latter to the former, as a mass proletarian movement and tried to draw practical lessons from it. He 'learned'
from the Commune, just as all the great revolutionary thinkers learned unhesitatingly from the experience of great
movements of the oppressed classes, and never addressed
them with pedantic 'homilies' (such as Plekhanov's 'They
should not have taken up arms', or Tsereteli's 'A class must
limit itself').

Abolishing the bureaucracy at once, everywhere and
completely, is out of the question. It is a utopia. But to *smash*
the old bureaucratic machine at once and to begin immediately to construct a new one that will make possible the gradual abolition of all bureaucracy – this is *not* a utopia, it is the
experience of the Commune, the direct and immediate task
of the revolutionary proletariat.

Capitalism simplifies the functions of 'state' administration; it makes it possible to cast 'bossing' aside and to confine the whole matter to the organization of the proletarians (as the ruling class), which will hire 'workers, foremen and accountants' in the name of the whole of society.

We are not utopians, we do not 'dream' of dispensing *at once* with all administration, with all subordination. These anarchist dreams, based upon incomprehension of the tasks of the proletarian dictatorship, are totally alien to Marxism, and, as a matter of fact, serve only to postpone the socialist revolution until people are different. No, we want the socialist revolution with people as they are now, with people who cannot dispense with subordination, control, and 'foremen and accountants'.

The subordination, however, must be to the armed vanguard of all the exploited and working people, i.e. to the proletariat. A beginning can and must be made at once, overnight, to replace the specific 'bossing' of state officials by the simple functions of 'foremen and accountants', functions which are already fully within the ability of the average town dweller and can well be performed for 'workmen's wages'.

We, the workers, shall organize large-scale production on the basis of what capitalism has already created, relying on our own experience as workers, establishing strict, iron discipline backed up by the state power of the armed workers. We shall reduce the role of state officials to that of simply carrying out our instructions as responsible, revocable, modestly paid 'foremen and accountants' (of course, with the aid of technicians of all sorts, types and degrees). This is *our* proletarian task, this is what we can and must *start* with in accomplishing the proletarian revolution. Such a beginning, on the basis of large-scale production, will of itself lead to the gradual 'withering away' of all bureaucracy, to the gradual creation of an order – an order without inverted commas, an order bearing no similarity to wage slavery – an order under which the functions of control and accounting, becoming more and more simple, will be performed by each in turn, will then become a habit and will finally die out as the *special* functions of a special section of the population.

A witty German Social Democrat of the 1870s called the *postal service* an example of the socialist economic system. This is very true. At the present, the postal service is a business organized on the lines of state-*capitalist* monopoly. Imperialism is gradually transforming all trusts into organizations of a similar type, in which, standing over the 'common' people, who are overworked and starved, one has the same bourgeois bureaucracy. But the mechanism of social management is here already to hand. Once we have overthrown the capitalists, crushed the resistance of these exploiters with the iron hand of the armed workers, and smashed the bureaucratic machinery of the modern state, we shall have a splendidly equipped mechanism, freed from the 'parasite', a mechanism which can very well be set going by the united workers themselves, who will hire technicians, foremen and accountants, and pay them *all*, as indeed *all* 'state' officials in general, workmen's wages. Here is a concrete, practical task which can immediately be fulfilled in relation to all trusts, a task whose fulfilment will rid the working people of exploitation, a task which takes account of what the Commune had already begun to practise (particularly in building up the state).

To organize the *whole* economy on the lines of the postal service so that the technicians, foremen and accountants, as well as *all* officials, shall receive salaries no higher than 'a workman's wage', all under the control and leadership of the armed proletariat – that is our immediate aim. This is what will bring about the abolition of parliamentarism and the preservation of representative institutions. This is what will rid the labouring classes of the bourgeoisie's prostitution of these institutions.

IV. Organization of National Unity

'In a brief sketch of national organization which the Commune had no time to develop, it states explicitly that the Commune was to be the political form of even the smallest village.' The communes were to elect the 'National Delegation' in Paris:

> The few but important functions which would still remain for a central government were not to be suppressed, as had been deliberately mis-stated, but were to be transferred to communal, i.e. strictly responsible, officials . . . National unity was not to be broken, but, on the contrary, organized by the communal

constitution; it was to become a reality by the destruction of state power which posed as the embodiment of that unity yet wanted to be independent of, and superior to, the nation, on whose body it was but a parasitic excrescence. While the merely repressive organs of the old governmental power were to be amputated, its legitimate functions were to be wrested from an authority claiming the right to stand above society, and restored to the responsible servants of society.

The extent to which the opportunists of present-day Social Democracy have failed – perhaps it would be more true to say, have refused – to understand these observations of Marx is best shown by that book of Herostratean fame of the renegade Bernstein, *The Premises of Socialism and the Tasks of the Social Democrats*. It is in connection with the above passage from Marx that Bernstein wrote that 'as far as its political content', this programme 'displays, in all its essential features, the greatest similarity to the federalism of Proudhon . . . In spite of all the other points of difference between Marx and the "petty-bourgeois" Proudhon [Bernstein places the word 'petty-bourgeois' in inverted commas, to make it sound ironical] on these points, their lines of reasoning run as close as could be.' Of course, Bernstein continues, the importance of the municipalities is growing, but 'it seems doubtful to me whether the first job of democracy would be such a dissolution [*Auflosung*] of the modern states and such a complete transformation [*Umwandlung*] of their organization as is visualized by Marx and Proudhon (the formation of a

National Assembly from delegates of the provincial of district assemblies, which, in their turn, would consist of delegates from the communes), so that consequently the previous mode of national representation would disappear' (Bernstein, *Premises*, German edition, 1899, pp. 134 and 136).

To confuse Marx's view on the 'destruction of state power, a parasitic excrescence', with Proudhon's federalism is positively monstrous! But it is no accident, for it never occurs to the opportunist that Marx does not speak here at all about federalism as opposed to centralism, but about smashing the old, bourgeois state machine which exists in all bourgeois countries.

The only thing that does occur to the opportunist is what he sees around him, in an environment of petty-bourgeois philistinism and 'reformists'' stagnation, namely, only 'municipalities'! The opportunist has even grown out of the habit of thinking about proletarian revolution.

It is ridiculous. But the remarkable thing is that nobody argued with Bernstein on this point. Bernstein has been refuted by many, especially by Plekhanov in Russian literature and by Kautsky in European literature, but neither of them has said *anything* about *this* distortion of Marx by Bernstein.

The opportunist has so much forgotten how to think in a revolutionary way and to dwell on revolution that he attributes 'federalism' to Marx, whom he confuses with the founder of anarchism, Proudhon. As for Kautsky and Plekhanov, who claim to be orthodox Marxists and defenders of the theory of revolutionary Marxism, they are silent on this point! Here is one of the roots of the extreme vulgarization of the views on the difference between Marxism and anarchism, which is characteristic of both the Kautskyites and the opportunists, and which we shall discuss again later.

There is not a trace of federalism in Marx's above-quoted observation on the experience of the Commune. Marx agreed with Proudhon on the very point that the opportunist Bernstein did not see. Marx disagreed with Proudhon on the very point on which Bernstein found a similarity between them.

Marx agreed with Proudhon in that they both stood for the 'smashing' of the modern state machine. Neither the opportunists nor the Kautskyites wish to see the similarity of views on this point between Marxism and anarchism (both Proudhon and Bakunin) because this is where they have departed from Marxism.

Marx disagreed both with Proudhon and Bakunin precisely on the question of federalism (not to mention the dictatorship of the proletariat). Federalism as a principle follows logically from the petty-bourgeois views of anarchism. Marx was a centralist. There is no departure whatever from centralism in his observations just quoted. Only those who are imbued with the philistine 'superstitious belief' in the state can mistake the destruction of the bourgeois state machine for the destruction of centralism!

Now, if the proletariat and the poor peasants take state power into their own hands, organize themselves quite freely in communes, and *unite* the action of all the communes in striking at capital, in crushing the resistance of the capitalists, and in transferring the privately owned railways, factories, land, and so on to the *entire* nation, to the whole of society, won't that be centralism? Won't that be the most consistent democratic centralism and, moreover, proletarian centralism?

Bernstein simply cannot conceive of the possibility of voluntary centralism, of the voluntary fusion of the proletarian communes, for the sole purpose of destroying bourgeois rule and the bourgeois state machine. Like all philistines, Bernstein pictures centralism as something which can be imposed and maintained solely from above, and solely by the bureaucracy and military clique.

As though foreseeing that his views might be distorted, Marx expressly emphasized that the charge that the Commune had wanted to destroy national unity, to abolish the central authority, was a deliberate fraud. Marx purposely used the words: 'National unity was . . . to be organized', so as to oppose conscious, democratic, proletarian centralism to bourgeois, military, bureaucratic centralism.

But there are none so deaf as those who will not hear. And the very thing the opportunists of present-day Social Democracy do not want to hear about it the destruction of state power, the amputation of the parasitic excrescence.

V. Abolition of the Parasite State

We have already quoted Marx's words on the subject, and we must now supplement them.

'It is generally the fate of new historical creations,' he wrote,

> to be mistaken for the counterpart of older and even defunct forms of social life, to which they may bear a certain likeness. Thus, this new Commune, which breaks [*bricht*, smashes] the modern state power, has been regarded as a revival of the medieval communes ... as a federation of small states (as Montesquieu and the Girondins visualized it)[9] ... as an exaggerated form of the old struggle against overcentralization ...
>
> The Communal Constitution would have restored to the social body all the forces hitherto absorbed by that parasitic excrescence, the 'state', feeding upon and hampering the free movement of society. By this one act it would have initiated the regeneration of France ...
>
> The Communal Constitution would have brought the rural producers under the intellectual lead of the central towns of their districts, and there secured to them, in the town working men, the natural trustees of their interests. The very existence of the Commune involved, as a matter of course, local self-government, but no longer as a counterpoise to state power, now become superfluous.

'Breaking state power', which was a 'parasitic excrescence'; its 'amputation', its 'smashing'; 'state power, now become superfluous' – these are the expressions Marx used in regard to the state when appraising and analysing the experience of the Commune.

All this was written a little less than half a century ago; and now one has to engage in excavations, as it were, in order to bring undistorted Marxism to the knowledge of the mass of the people. The conclusions drawn from the observation of the last great revolution which Marx lived through were forgotten just when the time for the next great proletarian revolution has arrived.

> The multiplicity of interpretations to which the Commune has been subjected, and the multiplicity of interests which expressed themselves in it show that it was a thoroughly flexible political form, while all previous forms of government had been essentially repressive. Its true secret was this: it was essentially a working-class government, the result of the struggle of the producing against the appropriating class, the political form at last discovered under which the economic emancipation of labour could be accomplished . . .
>
> Except on this last condition, the Communal Constitution would have been an impossibility and a delusion.

The utopians busied themselves with 'discovering' political forms under which the socialist transformation of society was to take place. The anarchists dismissed the question of political forms altogether. The opportunists of present-day Social Democracy accepted the bourgeois political forms of the parliamentary democratic state as the limit which should not be overstepped; they battered their foreheads praying before this 'model', and denounced as anarchism every desire to *break* these forms.

Marx deduced from the whole history of socialism and the political struggle that the state was bound to disappear, and that the transitional form of its disappearance (the transition from state to non-state) would be the 'proletariat organized as the ruling class'. Marx, however, did not set out to *discover* the political *forms* of this future stage. He limited himself to carefully observing French history, to analysing it, and to drawing the conclusion to which the year 1851 had led, namely, that matters were moving towards *destruction* of the bourgeois state machine.

And when the mass revolutionary movement of the proletariat burst forth, Marx, in spite of its failure, in spite of its short life and patent weakness, began to study the forms it had *discovered*.

The Commune is the form 'at last discovered' by the proletarian revolution, under which the economic emancipation of labour can take place.

The Commune is the first attempt by a proletarian revolution to *smash* the bourgeois state machine; and it is the political form 'at last discovered', by which the smashed state machine can and must be *replaced*.

We shall see further on that the Russian revolutions of 1905 and 1917, in different circumstances and under different conditions, continue the work of the Commune and confirm Marx's brilliant historical analysis.

4

SUPPLEMENTARY EXPLANATIONS BY ENGELS

Marx provided the fundamentals concerning the significance of the experience of the Commune. Engels returned to the same subject time and again, and explained Marx's analysis and conclusions, sometimes elucidating *other* aspects of the question with such power and vividness that it is necessary to deal with his explanations specially.

I. The Housing Question

In his work, *The Housing Question* (1872), Engels already took into account the experience of the Commune, and dealt several times with the tasks of the revolution in relation to the state. It is interesting to note that the treatment of this specific subject clearly revealed, on the one hand, points of similarity between the proletarian state and the present state – points that warrant speaking of the state in both cases – and, on the other hand, points of difference between them, or the transition to the destruction of the state.

> How is the housing question to be settled then? In present-day society, it is settled just as any other social question: by the gradual economic levelling of demand and supply, a settlement which reproduces the question itself again and again and therefore is no settlement. How a social revolution would settle this question not only depends on the circumstances in each particular case, but is also connected with much more far-reaching questions, one of the most fundamental of which is the abolition of the antithesis between town and country. As it is not our task to create utopian systems for the organization of the future society, it would be more than idle to go into the question here. But one thing is certain: there is already a sufficient quantity of houses in the big cities to remedy immediately all real 'housing shortage', provided they are used judiciously. This can naturally only occur through the expropriation of the present owners and by quartering in their houses homeless workers or workers overcrowded in their present homes. As soon as the proletariat has won political power, such a measure prompted by concern for the common good will be just as easy to carry out as are other expropriations and billetings by the present-day state.
>
> (German edition, 1887, p. 22)[1]

The change in the form of state power is not examined here, but only the content of its activity. Expropriations and billetings take place by order even of the present state. From the formal point of view, the proletarian state will also 'order' the occupation of dwellings and expropriation of houses. But it is clear that the old executive apparatus, the bureaucracy, which is connected with the bourgeoisie, would simply be unfit to carry out the orders of the proletarian state.

> It must be pointed out that the 'actual seizure' of all the instruments of labour, the taking possession of industry as a whole by the working people, is the exact opposite of the Proudhonist 'redemption'. In the latter case the individual worker becomes the owner of the dwelling, the peasant farm, the instruments of labour; in the former case, the 'working people' remain the collective owners of the houses, factories and instruments of labour, and will hardly permit their use, at least during a transitional period, by individuals or associations without compensation for the cost. In the same way, the abolition of property in land is not the abolition of ground rent but its transfer, if in a modified form, to society. The actual seizure of all the instruments of labour by the working people, therefore, does not at all preclude the retention of rent relations.
>
> (p. 68)

We shall examine the question touched upon in this passage, namely, the economic basis for the withering away of the state, in the next chapter. Engels expresses himself most cautiously, saying that the proletarian state would 'hardly' permit the use of houses without payment, 'at least during a transitional period'. The letting of houses owned by the whole people to individual families presupposes the collection of rent, a certain amount of control, and the employment of some standard in allotting the housing. All this calls for a certain form of state, but it does not at all call for a special military bureaucratic apparatus, with officials occupying especially privileged positions. The transition to a situation in which it will be possible to supply dwellings rent-free depends on the complete 'withering away' of the state.

Speaking of the Blanquists' adoption of the fundamental position of Marxism after the Commune and under the influence of its experience, Engels, in passing, formulates this position as follows:

> Necessity of political action by the proletariat and of its dictatorship as the transition to the abolition of classes and, with them, of the state.
>
> (p. 55)

Addicts of hair-splitting criticism, or bourgeois 'exterminators of Marxism', will perhaps see a contradiction between this *recognition* of the 'abolition of the state' and repudiation of this formula as an anarchist one in the above passage from *Anti-Dühring*. It would not be surprising if the opportunists classed Engels, too, as an 'anarchist', for it is becoming increasingly common with the social-chauvinists to accuse the internationalists of anarchism.

Marxism has always taught that with the abolition of classes the state will also be abolished. The well-known passage on the 'withering away of the state' in *Anti-Dühring* accuses the anarchists not simply of favouring the abolition of the state, but of preaching that the state can be abolished 'overnight'.

As the now prevailing 'Social-Democratic' doctrine completely distorts the relation of Marxism to anarchism on the question of the abolition of the state, it will be particularly useful to recall a certain controversy in which Marx and Engels came out against the anarchists.

II. Controversy with the Anarchists

This controversy took place in 1873. Marx and Engels contributed articles against the Proudhonists, 'autonomists' or 'anti-authoritarians', to an Italian socialist annual, and it was not until 1913 that these articles appeared in German in *Neue Zeit*.[2]

'If the political struggle of the working class assumes revolutionary form,' wrote Marx, ridiculing the anarchists for their repudiation of politics,

and if the workers set up their revolutionary dictatorship in place of the dictatorship of the bourgeoisie, they commit the terrible crime of violating principles, for in order to satisfy their wretched, vulgar everyday needs and to crush the resistance of

the bourgeoisie, they give the state a revolutionary and transient form, instead of laying down their arms and abolishing
the state.

(Neue Zeit, Vol. XXXII, 1, 1913–14, p. 40)

It was solely against this kind of 'abolition' of the state that
Marx fought in refuting the anarchists! He did not at all
oppose the view that the state would disappear when classes
disappeared, or that it would be abolished when classes were
abolished. What he did oppose was the proposition that the
workers should renounce the use of arms, organized violence,
that is, *the state*, which is to serve to 'crush the resistance of
the bourgeoisie'.

To prevent the true meaning of his struggle against anarchism from being distorted, Marx expressly emphasized the
'revolutionary and *transient* form' of the state which the proletariat needs. The proletariat needs the state only temporarily.
We do not after all differ with the *anarchists* on the question of
the abolition of the state as the *aim*. We maintain that, to achieve
this aim, we must temporarily make use of the instruments,
resources and methods of state power *against* the exploiters, just
as the temporary dictatorship of the oppressed class is necessary
for the abolition of classes. Marx chooses the sharpest and clear-
est way of stating his case against the anarchists. After overthrowing the yoke of the capitalists, should the workers 'lay
down their arms', or use them against the capitalists in order to
crush their resistance? But what is the systematic use of arms by
one class against another if not a 'transient form' of state?

Let every Social Democrat ask himself: is *that* how he has been posing the question of the state in controversy with the anarchists? Is *that* how it has been posed by the vast majority of the official socialist parties of the Second International?

Engels expounds the same ideas in much greater detail and still more popularly. First of all, he ridicules the muddled ideas of the Proudhonists, who call themselves 'anti-authoritarians', i.e. repudiated all authority, all subordination, all power. Take a factory, a railway, a ship on the high seas, said Engels: is it not clear that not one of these complex technical establishments, based on the use of machinery and the systematic co-operation of many people, could function without a certain amount of subordination and, consequently, without a certain amount of authority or power?

> When I counter the most rabid anti-authoritarians with these arguments, they only answer they can give me is the following. Oh, that's true, except that here it is not a question of authority with which we vest our delegates, *but of a commission!* These people imagine they can change a thing by changing its name.

Having thus shown that authority and autonomy are relative terms, that the sphere of their application varies with the various phases of social development, that it is absurd to take them as absolutes, and adding that the sphere of application of machinery and large-scale production is steadily expanding,

Engels passes from the general discussion of authority to the question of the state.

'Had the autonomists,' he wrote, 'contented themselves with saying that the social organization of the future would allow authority only within the bounds which the conditions of production make inevitable, one could have come to terms with them. But they are blind to all facts that make authority necessary and they passionately fight the word.'

Why do the anti-authoritarians not confine themselves to crying out against political authority, the state? All socialists are agreed that the state, and with it political authority, will disappear as a result of the coming social revolution, that is, that public functions will lose their political character and become mere administrative functions of watching over social interests. But the anti-authoritarians demand that the political state be abolished at one stroke, even before the social relations that gave both to it have been destroyed. They demand that the first act of the social revolution shall be the abolition of authority.

Have these gentlemen ever seen a revolution? A revolution is certainly the most authoritarian thing there is; it is an act whereby one part of the population imposes its will upon the other part by means of rifles, bayonets and cannon, all of which are highly authoritarian means. And the victorious party must maintain its rule by means of the terror which its arms inspire in the reactionaries. Would the Paris Commune have lasted more than a day if it had not used the authority of the armed people against the bourgeoisie? Cannot we, on the contrary, blame it for having made too little use of that authority? Therefore, one of two things: either that anti-authoritarians don't know what they are talking about, in which case they are creating nothing but confusion. Or they do know, and in that case they are betraying the cause of the proletariat. In either case they serve only reaction.

(p. 39)

This argument touches upon questions which should be examined in connection with the relationship between politics and economics during the withering away of the state (the next chapter is devoted to this). These questions are: the transformation of public functions from political into simple functions of administration, and the 'political state'. This last term, one particularly liable to misunderstanding, indicates the process of the withering away of the state: at a certain stage of this process, the state which is withering away may be called a non-political state.

Again, the most remarkable thing in this argument of Engels is the way he states his case against the anarchists. Social Democrats, claiming to be disciples of Engels, have argued on this subject against the anarchists millions of times since 1873, but they have *not* argued as Marxists could and should. The anarchist idea of abolition of the state is muddled and *non-revolutionary* – that is how Engels put it. It is precisely the revolution in its rise and development, with its specific tasks in relation to violence, authority, power, the state, that the anarchists refuse to see.

The usual criticism of anarchism by present-day Social Democrats has boiled down to the purest philistine banality: 'We recognize the state, whereas the anarchists do not!' Naturally, such banality cannot but repel workers who are at all capable of thinking and revolutionary-minded. What Engels says is different. He stresses that all socialists recognize that the state will disappear as a result of the socialist revolution. He then deals specifically with the question of the revolution – the very question which, as a rule, the Social Democrats evade out of opportunism, leaving it, so to speak, exclusively for the anarchists 'to work out'. And when dealing with this question, Engels takes the bull by the horns; he asks: should not the Commune have made *more* use of the *revolutionary* power of the *state*, that is, of the proletariat armed and organized as the ruling class?

Prevailing official Social Democracy usually dismissed the question of the concrete tasks of the proletariat in the revolution either with a philistine sneer, or, at best, with the sophistic evasion: 'The future will show.' And the anarchists were justified in saying about such Social Democrats that they were failing in their task of giving the workers a revolutionary education. Engels draws upon the experience of the last proletarian revolution precisely for the purpose of making a most concrete study of what should be done by the proletariat, and in what manner, in relation to both the banks and the state.

III. Letter to Bebel

One of the most, if not the most, remarkable observations on the state in the works of Marx and Engels is contained in the following passage in Engels's letter to Bebel dated 18–28 March 1875.[3] This letter, we may observe in parenthesis, was, as far as we know, first published by Bebel in the second volume of his memoirs (*From My Life*), which appeared in 1911, i.e. thirty-six years after the letter had been written and sent.

Engels wrote to Bebel criticizing the same draft of the Gotha Programme which Marx criticized in his famous letter to Bracke.[4] Referring specially to the question of the state, Engels said:

> The free people's state has been transferred into the free state. Taken in its grammatical sense, a free state is one where the state is free in relation to its citizens, hence a state with a despotic government. The whole talk about the state should be dropped, especially since the Commune, which was no longer a state in the proper sense of the word. The 'people's state' has been thrown in our faces by the anarchists to the point of disgust, although already Marx's book against Proudhon and later the *Communist Manifesto* say plainly that with the introduction of the socialist order of society the state dissolves of itself [*sich auflöst*] and disappears. As the state is only a transitional institution which is used in the struggle, in the revolution, to hold down one's adversaries by force, it is sheer nonsense to talk of

a 'free people's state'; so long as the proletariat still *needs* the state, it does not need it in the interests of freedom but in order to hold down its adversaries, and as soon as it becomes possible to speak of freedom the state as such ceases to exist. We would therefore propose replacing the *state* everywhere by *Gemeinwesen*, a good old German word which can very well take the place of the French word commune.

(pp. 321–2 of the German original)[5]

It should be borne in mind that this letter refers to the party programme which Marx criticized in a letter dated only a few weeks later than the above (Marx's letter is dated 5 May 1875), and that, at the time, Engels was living with Marx in London. Consequently, when he says 'we' in the last sentence, Engels undoubtedly, in his own as well as in Marx's name, suggests to the leader of the German workers' party that the word 'state' *be struck out of the programme* and replaced by the word *'community'*.

What a howl about 'anarchism' would be raised by the leading lights of present-day 'Marxism', which has been falsified for the convenience of the opportunists, if such an amendment of the programme were suggested to them!

Let them howl. This will earn them the praises of the bourgeoisie.

And we shall go on with our work. In revising the programme of our Party, we must by all means take the advice of Engels and Marx into consideration in order to come nearer the truth, to restore Marxism by ridding it of distortions, to guide the struggle of the working class for its emancipation more correctly. Certainly no one opposed to the advice of Engels and Marx will be found among the Bolsheviks. The only difficulty that may perhaps arise will be in regard to the term. In German there are two words meaning 'community', of which Engels used the one which does *not* denote a single community, but their totality, a system of communities. In Russian there is no such word, and we may have to choose the French word 'commune', although this also has its drawbacks.

'The Commune was no longer a state in the proper sense of the word' – this is the most theoretically important statement Engels makes. After what has been said above, this statement is perfectly clear. The Commune *was ceasing* to be a state since it had to suppress, not the majority of the population, but a minority (the exploiters). It had smashed the bourgeois state machine. In place of a *special* coercive force the population itself came on the scene. All this was a departure from the state in the proper sense of the word. And had the Commune become firmly established, all traces of the state in it would have 'withered away' of themselves; it would not have had to 'abolish' the institutions of the state – they would have ceased to function as they ceased to have anything to do.

'The "people's state" has been thrown in our faces by the anarchists.' In saying this, Engels above all has in mind Bakunin[6] and his attacks on the German Social Democrats. Engels admits that these attacks were justified *insofar as* the 'people's state' was as much an absurdity and as much a departure from socialism as the 'free people's state'. Engels tried to put the struggle of the German Social Democrats against the anarchists on the right lines, to make this struggle correct in principle, to ride it of opportunist prejudices concerning the 'state'. Unfortunately, Engels's letter was pigeon-holed for thirty-six years. We shall see farther on that, even after this letter was published, Kautsky persisted in virtually the same mistakes against which Engels had warned.

Bebel replied to Engels in a letter dated 21 September 1875, in which he wrote, among other things, that he 'fully agreed' with Engels's opinion of the draft programme, and that he had reproached Liebknecht with readiness to make concessions (p. 334 of the German edition of Bebel's memoirs, Vol. II). But if we take Bebel's pamphlet, *Our Aims*, we find there views on the state that are absolutely wrong:

> The state must . . . be transformed from one based on class rule into a people's state.
>
> (*Unsere Ziele*, 1886, p. 14)

This was printed in the ninth (ninth!) edition of Bebel's pamphlet! It is not surprising that opportunist views on the state, so persistently repeated, were absorbed by the German Social Democrats, especially as Engels's revolutionary interpretations had been safely pigeon-holed, and all the conditions of life were such as to 'wean' them from revolution for a long time.

IV. Criticism of the Draft of the Erfurt Programme

In analysing Marxist teachings on the state, the criticism of the draft of the Erfurt Programme, sent by Engels to Kautsky on 29 June 1891, and published only ten years later in *Neue Zeit*, cannot be ignored; for it is with the *opportunist* views of the Social Democrats on questions of *state* organization that this criticism is mainly concerned.[7]

We shall note in passing that Engels also makes an exceedingly valuable observation on economic questions, which shows how attentively and thoughtfully he watched the various changes occurring in modern capitalism, and how for this reason he was able to foresee to a certain extent the tasks of our present, the imperialist, epoch. Here is that observation: referring to the word 'planlessness' (*Planlosigkeit*), used in the draft programme, as characteristic of capitalism, Engels wrote:

> When we pass from joint-stock companies to trusts which assume control over, and monopolize, whole industries, it is not only private production that ceases, but also planlessness.
>
> (*Neue Zeit*, Vol. XX, 1, 1901–2, p. 8)

Here we have what is most essential in the theoretical appraisal of the latest phase of capitalism, i.e. imperialism, namely, that capitalism becomes monopoly *capitalism*. The latter must be emphasized because the erroneous bourgeois reformist assertion that monopoly capitalism or state-monopoly capitalism is no longer capitalism, but can now be called 'state socialism' and so on, is very common. The trusts, of course, never provided, do not now provide, and cannot provide complete planning. But however much they do plan, however much the capitalist magnates calculate in advance the volume of production on a national and even on an international scale, and however much they systematically regulate it, we still remain under *capitalism* – at its new stage, it is true, but still capitalism, without a doubt. The 'proximity' of *such* capitalism to socialism should serve genuine representatives of the proletariat as an argument proving the proximity, facility, feasibility and urgency of the socialist revolution, and not at all as an argument for tolerating the repudiation of such a revolution and the efforts to make capitalism look more attractive, something which all reformists are trying to do.

But to return to the question of the state. In his letter, Engels makes three particularly valuable suggestions: first, in regard to the republic; second, in regard to the connection between the national question and state organization; and, third, in regard to local self-government.

Regarding the republic, Engels made this the focal point of this criticism of the draft of the Erfurt Programme. And when we recall the importance which the Erfurt Programme acquired for all the Social Democrats of the world, and that it became the model for the whole Second International, we may say without exaggeration that Engels thereby criticizes the opportunism of the whole Second International: 'The political demands of the draft,' Engels wrote, 'have one great fault. *It lacks* [Engels's italics] precisely what should have been said.'

And, later on, he makes it clear that the German Constitution is, strictly speaking, a copy of the extremely reactionary Constitution of 1850, that the Reichstag is only, as Wilhelm Liebknecht[8] put it, 'the fig leaf of absolutism' and that to wish 'to transform all the instruments of labour into common property' on the basis of a constitution which legalizes the existence of petty states and the federation of petty German states is an 'obvious absurdity'.

'To touch on that is dangerous, however,' Engels added, knowing only too well that it was impossible legally to include in the programme the demand for a republic in Germany. But he refused to merely accept this obvious consideration which satisfied 'everybody'. He continued:

> Nevertheless, somehow or other, the thing has to be attacked. How necessary this is is shown precisely at the present time by opportunism, which is gaining ground [*einreissende*] in a large section of the Social-Democrat press. Fearing a renewal of the Anti-Socialist Law,[9] or recalling all manner of overhasty pronouncements made during the reign of that law, they now want the Party to find the present legal order in Germany adequate for putting through all Party demands by peaceful means.

Engels particularly stressed the fundamental fact that the German Social Democrats were prompted by fear of a renewal of the Anti-Socialist Law, and explicitly described it as opportunism; he declared that precisely because there was no republic and no freedom in Germany, the dreams of a 'peaceful' path were perfectly absurd. Engels was careful not to tie his hands. He admitted that in republican or very free countries 'one can conceive' (only 'conceive'!) of a peaceful development towards socialism, but in Germany, he repeated,

> in Germany, where the government is almost omnipotent and the Reichstag and all other representative bodies have no real power, to advocate such a thing in Germany, where, moreover, there is no need to do so, means removing the fig leaf from absolutism and becoming oneself a screen for its nakedness.

The great majority of the official leaders of the German Social-Democratic Party, which pigeon-holed this advice, have really proved to be a screen for absolutism.

> In the long run such a policy can only lead one's own party astray. They push general, abstract political questions into the foreground, thereby concealing the immediate concrete questions, which at the moment of the first great events, the first political crisis, automatically pose themselves. What can result from this except that at the decisive moment the party suddenly proves helpless and that uncertainty and discord on the most decisive issues reign in it because these issues have never been discussed? . . .

This forgetting of the great, the principal considerations for the momentary interests of the day, this struggling and striving for the success of the moment regardless of later consequences, this sacrifice of the future of the movement for its present may be 'honestly' meant, but it is and remains opportunism, and 'honest' opportunism is perhaps the most dangerous of all . . .

If one thing is certain it is that our party and the working class can only come to power in the form of the democratic republic. This is even the specific form for the dictatorship of the proletariat, as the Great French Revolution has already shown.

Engels realized here in a particularly striking form the fundamental idea which runs through all of Marx's works, namely, that the democratic republic is the nearest approach to the dictatorship of the proletariat. For such a republic, without in the least abolishing the rule of capital, and, therefore, the oppression of the masses and the class struggle, inevitably leads to such an extension, development, unfolding, and intensification of this struggle that, as soon as it becomes possible to meet the fundamental interests of the oppressed masses, this possibility is realized inevitably and solely through the dictatorship of the proletariat, through the leadership of those masses by the proletariat. These, too, are 'forgotten words' of Marxism for the whole of the Second International, and the fact that they have been forgotten was demonstrated with particular vividness by the history of the

Menshevik Party during the first six months of the Russian revolution of 1917.

On the subject of a federal republic, in connection with the national composition of the population, Engels wrote:

> What should take the place of the present-day Germany [with its reactionary monarchical Constitution and its equally reactionary division into petty states, a division which perpetuates all the specific features of 'Prussianism' instead of dissolving them in Germany as a whole]? In my view, the proletariat can only use the form of the one and indivisible republic. In the gigantic territory of the United States, a federal republic is still, on the whole, a necessity, although in the Eastern states it is already becoming a hindrance. It would be a step forward in Britain where the two islands are peopled by four nations and in spite of a single Parliament three different systems of legislation already exist side by side. In little Switzerland, it has long been a hindrance, tolerable only because Switzerland is content to be a purely passive member of the European state system. For Germany, federalization on the Swiss model would be an enormous step backward. Two points distinguish a union state from a completely unified state: first, that each member state, each canton, has its own civil and criminal legislative and judicial system, and, second, that alongside a popular chamber there is also a federal chamber in which each canton, whether large or small, votes as such.
>
> In Germany, the union state is the transition to the completely unified state, and the 'revolution from above' of 1866 and 1870

must not be reversed but supplemented by a 'movement from below'.

Far from being indifferent to the forms of state, Engels, on the contrary, tried to analyse the transitional forms with the utmost thoroughness in order to establish, in accordance with the concrete historical peculiarities of each particular case, *from what and to what* the given transitional form is passing.

Approaching the matter from the standpoint of the proletariat and the proletarian revolution, Engels, like Marx, upheld democratic centralism, the republic – one and indivisible. He regarded the federal republic either as an exception and a hindrance to development, or as a transition from a monarchy to a centralized republic, as a 'step forward' under certain special conditions. And, among these special conditions, he puts the national question to the fore.

Although mercilessly criticizing the reactionary nature of small states, and the screening of this by the national question in certain concrete cases, Engels, like Marx, never betrayed the slightest desire to brush aside the national question – a desire of which the Dutch and Polish Marxists, who proceed from their perfectly justified opposition to the narrow philistine nationalism of 'their' little states, are often guilty.

Even in regard to Britain, where geographical conditions, a common language and the history of many centuries would seem to have 'put an end' to the national question in the various small divisions of the country – even in regard to that country, Engels reckoned with the plain fact that the national question was not yet a thing of the past, and recognized in consequence that the establishment of a federal republic would be a 'step forward'. Of course, there is not the slightest hint here of Engels abandoning the criticism of the shortcomings of a federal republic or renouncing the most determined advocacy of, and struggle for, a unified and centralized democratic republic.

But Engels did not at all mean democratic centralism in the bureaucratic sense in which the term is used by bourgeois and petty-bourgeois ideologists, the anarchists among the latter. His idea of centralism did not in the least preclude such broad local self-government as would combine the voluntary defence of the unity of the state by the 'communes' and districts, and the complete elimination of all bureaucratic practices and all 'ordering' from above. Carrying forward the programmatic views of Marxism on the state, Engels wrote:

So, then, a unified republic – but not in the sense of the present French Republic, which is nothing but the Empire established in 1798 without the Emperor. From 1792 to 1798 each French department, each commune [*Gemeinde*], enjoyed complete self-government on the American model, and this is what we too must have. How self-government is to be organized and how we can manage, without a bureaucracy has been shown to us by America and the first French Republic, and is being shown even today by Australia, Canada and the other English colonies. And a provincial [regional] and communal self-government of this type is far freer than, for instance, Swiss federalism, under which, it is true, the canton is very independent in relation to the Bund [i.e. the federated state as a whole], but is also independent in relation to the district [*Bezirk*] and the commune. The cantonal governments appoint the district governors [*Bezirksstatthalter*] and prefects – which is unknown in English-speaking countries and which we want to abolish here as resolutely in the future as the Prussian *Landräte* and *Regierungsräte* [commissioners, district police chiefs, governors, and in general all officials appointed from above].

Accordingly, Engels proposes the following words for the self-government clause in the programme: 'Complete self-government for the provinces [*gubernias* or regions], districts and communes through officials elected by universal suffrage. The abolition of all local and provincial authorities appointed by the state.'

I have already had occasion to point out – in *Pravda* (No. 68, 28 May 1917), which was suppressed by the government of Kerensky and other 'socialist' ministers – how, on this point (of course, not on this point alone by any means) our pseudo-socialist representatives of pseudo-revolutionary pseudo-democracy have made glaring departures *from democracy*. Naturally, people who have bound themselves by a 'coalition' to the imperialist bourgeoisie have remained deaf to this criticism.

It is extremely important to note that Engels, armed with facts, disproved by a most precise example the prejudice which is very widespread, particularly among petty-bourgeois democrats, that a federal republic necessarily means a greater amount of freedom than a centralized republic. This is wrong. It is disproved by the facts cited by Engels regarding the centralized French Republic of 1792–9 and the federal Swiss Republic. The really democratic centralized republic gave *more* freedom than the federal republic. In other words, the *greatest* amount of local, regional and other freedom known in history was accorded by a *centralized* and not a federal republic.

Insufficient attention has been and is being paid in our Party propaganda and agitation to this fact, as, indeed, to the whole question of the federal and the centralized republic and local self-government.

V. The 1891 Preface to Marx's *The Civil War in France*

In his preface to the third edition of *The Civil War in France* (this preface is dated 18 March 1891, and was originally published in *Neue Zeit*), Engels, in addition to some interesting incidental remarks on questions concerning the attitude towards the state, gave a remarkably vivid summary of the lessons of the Commune.[10] This summary, made more profound by the entire experience of the twenty years that separated the author from the Commune, and directed expressly against the 'superstitious belief in the state' so widespread in Germany, may justly be called the *last word* of Marxism on the question under consideration.

In France, Engels observed, the workers emerged with arms from every revolution: 'therefore the disarming of the workers was the first commandment for the bourgeois, who were at the helm of the state. Hence, after every revolution won by the workers, a new struggle, ending with the defeat of the workers.'

This summary of the experience of bourgeois revolutions is as concise as it is expressive. The essence of the matter – among other things, on the question of the state (has the oppressed class arms?) – is, here, remarkably well grasped. It is precisely this essence that is most often evaded by both professors influenced by bourgeois ideology, and by petty-bourgeois democrats. In the Russian revolution of 1917, the honour (Cavaignac honour)[11] of blabbing this secret of bourgeois revolutions fell to the Menshevik, would-be Marxist, Tsereteli. In his 'historic' speech of 11 June, Tsereteli blurted out that the bourgeoisie were determined to disarm the Petrograd workers – presenting, of course, this decision as his own, and as a necessity for the 'state' in general!

Tsereteli's historical speech of 11 June will, of course, serve every historian of the revolution of 1917 as a graphic illustration of how the Socialist-Revolutionary and Menshevik bloc, led by Mr Tsereteli, deserted to the bourgeoisie *against* the revolutionary proletariat.

Another incidental remark of Engels's, also connected with the question of the state, deals with religion. It is well known that the German Social Democrats, as they degenerated and became increasingly opportunist, slipped more and more frequently into the philistine misinterpretation of the celebrated formula: 'Religion is to be declared a private matter.' That is, the formula was twisted to mean that religion was a private matter *even for the party* of the revolutionary proletariat!! It was against this complete betrayal of the revolutionary programme of the proletariat that Engels vigorously protested. In 1891, he saw only the *very feeble* beginnings of opportunism in his party, and, therefore, he expressed himself with extreme caution:

> As almost only workers, or recognized representatives of the workers, sat in the Commune, its decisions bore a decidedly proletarian character. Either they decreed reforms which the republican bourgeoisie had failed to pass solely out of cowardice, but which provided a necessary basis for the free activity of the working class – such as the realization of the principle that *in relation to the state* religion is a purely private matter – or the Commune promulgated decrees which were in the direct interest of the working class and in part cut deeply into the old order of society.

Engels deliberately emphasized the words 'in relation to the state' as a straight thrust at German opportunism, which had declared religion to be a private matter *in relation to the party*, thus degrading the party of the revolutionary proletariat to the level of the most vulgar 'free-thinking' philistinism, which is prepared to allow a non-denominational status, but which renounces the *party* struggle against the opium of religion which stupefies the people.

The future historian of the German Social Democrats, in tracing the roots of their shameful bankruptcy in 1914, will find a fair amount of interesting material on this question, beginning with the evasive declarations in the articles of the party's ideological leader, Kautsky, which throw the door wide open to opportunism, and ending with the attitude of the party towards the 'Los-von-Kirche-Bewegung' (Leave-the-Church movement) in 1913.[12]

But let us see how, twenty years after the Commune, Engels summed up its lessons for the fighting proletariat.

Here are the lessons to which Engels attached prime importance:

It was precisely the oppressing power of the former centralized government, army, political parties, bureaucracy, which Napoleon had created in 1798 and which every new government had since then taken over as a welcome instrument and used against its opponents – it was this power which was to fall everywhere, just as it had fallen in Paris.

From the very outset the Commune had to recognize that the working class, once in power, could not go on managing with the old state machine; that in order not to lose again its only just-gained supremacy, this working class must, on the one hand, do away with all the old machinery of oppression previously used against it itself, and, on the other, safeguard itself

against its own deputies and officials, by declaring them all,
without exception, subject to recall at any time.

Engels emphasized once again that, not only under a monarchy but *also under a democratic republic*, the state remains a
state, i.e. it retains its fundamental distinguishing feature of
transforming the officials, the 'servants of society', its organs,
into the *masters* of society.

> Against this transformation of the state and the organs of the
> state from servants of society into masters of society – an
> inevitable transformation in all previous states — the
> Commune used two infallible means. In the first place, it filled
> all posts – administrative, judicial and educational – by elec-
> tion on the basis of universal suffrage of all concerned, subject
> to recall at any time by the electors. And, in the second place,
> it paid all officials, high or low, only the wages received by
> other workers. The highest salary paid by the Commune to
> anyone was 6,000 francs. In this way a dependable barrier to
> place-hunting and careerism was set up, even apart from the
> binding mandates to delegates to representative bodies, which
> were added besides.

Engels here approached the interesting boundary line at which
consistent democracy, on the one hand, is *transformed* into
socialism and, on the other, *demands* socialism. For, in order
to abolish the state, it is necessary to convert the functions of
the civil service into the simple operations of control and

accounting that are within the scope and ability of the vast majority of the population, and, subsequently, of every single individual. And if careerism is to be abolished completely, it must be made *impossible* for 'honourable' though profitless posts in the civil service to be used as a springboard to highly lucrative posts in banks or joint-stock companies, as *constantly* happens in all the freest capitalist countries.

Engels, however, did not make the mistake some Marxists make in dealing, for example, with the question of the right of nations to self-determination, when they argue that it is impossible under capitalism and will be superfluous under socialism. This seemingly clever but actually incorrect statement might be made in regard to *any* democratic institution, including moderate salaries for officials, because fully consistent democracy is impossible under capitalism, and, under socialism, all democracy will *wither away*.

This is a sophism like the old joke about a man becoming bald by losing one more hair.

To develop democracy *to the utmost*, to find *the forms* for this development, to test them *by practice*, and so forth – all this is one of the component tasks of the struggle for the social revolution. Taken separately, no kind of democracy will bring socialism. But, in actual life, democracy will never be 'taken separately'; it will be 'taken together' with other things, it will exert its influence on economic life as well, will stimulate *its* transformation; and in its turn it will be influenced by economic development, and so on. This is the dialectics of living history.

Engels continued:

This shattering [*Sprengung*] of the former state power and its replacement by a new and truly democratic one is described in detail in the third section of *The Civil War*. But it was necessary to touch briefly here once more on some of its features, because in Germany particularly the superstitious belief in the state has passed from philosophy into the general consciousness of the bourgeoisie and even of many workers. According to the philosophical conception, the state is the 'realization of the idea', or the Kingdom of God on earth, translated into philosophical terms, the sphere in which eternal truth and justice are, or should be, realized. And from this follows a superstitious reverence for the state and everything connected with it, which takes root the more readily since people are accustomed from childhood to imagine that the affairs and interests common to the whole of society could not be looked after other than as they have been looked after in the past, that is, through the state and its lucratively positioned officials. And people think they have taken quite an extraordinary bold step forward when they have rid themselves of belief in hereditary monarchy and swear by the democratic republic. In reality, however, the state is nothing but a machine for the oppression of one class by another, and indeed in the democratic republic no less than in the monarchy. And, at best, it is an evil inherited by the proletariat after its victorious struggle for class supremacy, whose worst sides the victorious proletariat will have to lop off as speedily as possible, just as the Commune had to, until a generation reared

in new, free social conditions is able to discard the entire lumber
of the state.

Engels warned the Germans not to forget the principles of
socialism with regard to the state in general in connection with
the substitution of a republic for the monarchy. His warnings
now read like a veritable lesson to the Tseretelis and Chernovs,
who in their 'coalition' practice have revealed a superstitious
belief in, and a superstitious reverence for, the state!

Two more remarks. First, Engels's statement that in a
democratic republic, 'no less' than in a monarchy, the state
remains a 'machine for the oppression of one class by another'
by no means signifies that the *form* of oppression makes no
difference to the proletariat, as some anarchists 'teach'. A
wider, freer and more open *form* of the class struggle and of
class oppression vastly assists the proletariat in its struggle
for the abolition of classes in general.

Second, why will only a new generation be able to discard
the entire lumber of the state? This question is bound up with
that of overcoming democracy, with which we shall deal now.

VI. Engels on the Overcoming of Democracy

Engels came to express his views on this subject when establishing that the term 'Social Democrat' was *scientifically*
wrong.

In a preface to an edition of his articles of the 1870s on
various subjects, mostly on 'international' questions

(*Internationales aus dem Volkstaat*), dated 3 January 1894, i.e. written a year and a half before his death, Engels wrote that in all his articles he used the word 'Communist', *and not* 'Social Democrat', because, at that time, the Proudhonists in France and the Lassalleans in Germany called themselves Social Democrats.[13]

'For Marx and myself,' continued Engels,

> it was therefore absolutely impossible to use such a loose term to characterize our special point of view. Today things are different, and the word ['Social Democrat'] may perhaps pass muster [*mag passieren*], inexact [*unpassend*, unsuitable] though it still is for a party whose economic programme is not merely socialist in general, but downright communist, and whose ultimate political aim is to overcome the whole state and, consequently, democracy as well. The names of *real* political parties, however, are never wholly appropriate; the party develops while the name stays.[14]

The dialectician Engels remained true to dialectics to the end of his days. Marx and I, he said, had a splendid, scientifically exact name for the party, but there was no real party, i.e. no mass proletarian party. Now (at the end of the nineteenth century) there was a real party, but its name was scientifically wrong. Never mind, it would 'pass muster', so long as the party *developed*, so long as the scientific in accuracy of the name was not hidden from it and did not hinder its development on the right direction!

Perhaps some wit would console us Bolsheviks in the manner of Engels: we have a real party, it is developing splendidly; even such a meaningless and ugly term as 'Bolshevik' will 'pass muster', although it expresses nothing whatever but the purely accidental fact that at the Brussels–London Congress of 1903 we were in the majority. Perhaps now that the persecution of our party by republicans and 'revolutionary' petty-bourgeois democrats in July and August has earned the name 'Bolshevik' such universal respect, now that, in addition, this persecution marks the tremendous historical progress our party has made in its *real* development – perhaps now even I might hesitate to insist on the suggestion I made in April to change the name of our party. Perhaps I would propose a 'compromise' to my comrades, namely, to call ourselves the Communist Party, but to retain the word 'Bolshevik' in brackets.

But the question of the name of the party is incomparably less important than the question of the attitude of the revolutionary proletariat to the state.

In the usual argument about the state, the mistake is constantly made against which Engels warned and which we have in passing indicated above, namely, it is constantly forgotten that the abolition of the state means also the abolition of democracy; that the withering away of the state means the withering away of democracy.

At first sight this assertion seems exceedingly strange and incomprehensible; indeed, someone may even suspect us of expecting the advent of a system of society in which the principle of subordination of the minority to the majority will not be observed – for democracy means the recognition of this very principle.

No, democracy is *not* identical with the subordination of the minority to the majority. Democracy is a *state* which recognizes the subordination of the minority to the majority, i.e. an organization for the systematic use of *force* by one class against another, by one section of the population against another.

We set ourselves the ultimate aim of abolishing the state, i.e. all organized and systematic violence, all use of violence against people in general. We do not expect the advent of a system of society in which the principle of subordination of the minority to the majority will not be observed. In striving for socialism, however, we are convinced that it will develop into communism and, therefore, that the need for violence against people in general, for the *subordination* of one man to another, and of one section of the population to another, will vanish altogether since people will *become accustomed* to observing the elementary conditions of social life *without violence* and *without subordination*.

In order to emphasize this element of habit, Engels speaks of a new *generation*, 'reared in new, free social conditions', which will 'be able to discard the entire lumber of the state' – of any state, including the democratic-republican state.

In order to explain this, it is necessary to analyse the economic basis of the withering away of the state.

5
THE ECONOMIC BASIS OF THE WITHERING AWAY OF THE STATE

Marx explains this question most thoroughly in his *Critique of the Gotha Programme* (letter to Bracke, 5 May 1875, which was not published until 1891 when it was printed in *Die Neue Zeit*, vol. IX, 1, and which has appeared in Russian in a special edition). The polemical part of this remarkable work, which contains a criticism of Lassalleanism, has, so to speak, overshadowed its positive part, namely, the analysis of the connection between the development of communism and the withering away of the state.

I. Presentation of the Question by Marx

From a superficial comparison of Marx's letter to Bracke of 5 May 1875, with Engels's letter to Bebel of 28 March 1875, which we examined above, it might appear that Marx was much more of a 'champion of the state' than Engels, and that the difference of opinion between the two writers on the question of the state was very considerable.

Engels suggested to Bebel that all chatter about the state be dropped altogether, that the word 'state' be eliminated from the programme entirely and the word 'community' substituted for it. Engels even declared that the Commune was no longer a state in the proper sense of the word. Yet Marx even spoke of the 'future state in communist society', i.e. he would seem to recognize the need for the state even under communism.

But such a view would be fundamentally wrong. A closer examination shows that Marx's and Engels's views on the state and its withering away were completely identical, and that Marx's expression quoted above refers to the state in the process of *withering away*.

Clearly, there can be no question of specifying the moment of the *future* 'withering away', the more so since it will obviously be a lengthy process. The apparent difference between Marx and Engels is due to the fact that they dealt with different subjects and pursued different aims. Engels set out to show Bebel graphically, sharply, and in broad outline the utter absurdity of the current prejudices concerning the state (shared to no small degree by Lassalle). Marx only touched upon *this* question in passing, being interested in another subject, namely, the *development* of communist society.

The whole theory of Marx is the application of the theory of development – in its most consistent, complete, considered and pithy form – to modern capitalism. Naturally, Marx was faced with the problem of applying this theory both to the *forthcoming* collapse of capitalism and to the *future* development of *future* communism.

On the basis of what *facts*, then, can the question of the future development of future communism be dealt with?

On the basis of the fact that it has its *origin* in capitalism, that it develops historically from capitalism, that it is the result of the action of a social force to which capitalism *gave birth*. There is no trace of an attempt on Marx's part to make up a utopia, to indulge in idle guesswork about what cannot be known. Marx treated the question of communism in the same way as a naturalist would treat the question of the development of, say, a new biological variety, once he knew that it had originated in such and such a way and was changing in such and such a definite direction.

To begin with, Marx brushed aside the confusion the Gotha Programme brought into the question of the relationship between state and society. He wrote:

'Present-day society' is capitalist society, which exists in all civilized countries, being more or less free from medieval admixture, more or less modified by the particular historical development of each country, more or less developed. On the other hand, the 'present-day state' changes with a country's frontier. It is different in the Prusso-German Empire from what it is in Switzerland, and different in England from what it is in the United States. 'The present-day state' is, therefore, a fiction.

Nevertheless, the different states of the different civilized countries, in spite of their motley diversity of form, all have this in common, that they are based on modern bourgeois society, only one more or less capitalistically developed. They have, therefore, also certain essential characteristics in common. In this sense it is possible to speak of the 'present-day state', in contrast with the future, in which its present root, bourgeois society, will have died off.

The question then arises: what transformation will the state undergo in communist society? In other words, what social functions will remain in existence there that are analogous to present state functions? This question can only be answered scientifically, and one does not get a flea-hop nearer to the problem by a thousandfold combination of the word people with the word state.[1]

After thus ridiculing all talk about a 'people's state', Marx formulated the question and gave warning, as it were, that those seeking a scientific answer to it should use only firmly established scientific data.

The first fact that has been established most accurately by the whole theory of development, by science as a whole – a fact that was ignored by the utopians, and is ignored by the present-day opportunists, who are afraid of the socialist revolution – is that, historically, there must undoubtedly be a special stage, or a special phase, of *transition* from capitalism to communism.

II. The Transition from Capitalism to Communism

Marx continued:

Between capitalist and communist society lies the period of the revolutionary transformation of the one into the other.

> Corresponding to this is also a political transition period in which the state can be nothing but the *revolutionary dictatorship of the proletariat*.

Marx bases this conclusion on an analysis of the role played by the proletariat in modern capitalist society, on the data concerning the development of this society, and on the irreconcilability of the antagonistic interests of the proletariat and the bourgeoisie.

Previously the question was put as follows: to achieve its emancipation, the proletariat must overthrow the bourgeoisie, win political power and establish its revolutionary dictatorship.

Now the question is put somewhat differently: the transition from capitalist society – which is developing towards communism – to communist society is impossible without a 'political transition period', and the state in this period can only be the revolutionary dictatorship of the proletariat.

What, then, is the relation of this dictatorship to democracy?

We have seen that the *Communist Manifesto* simply places side by side the two concepts: 'to raise the proletariat to the position of the ruling class' and 'to win the battle of democracy'. On the basis of all that has been said above, it is possible to determine more precisely how democracy changes in the transition from capitalism to communism.

In capitalist society, providing it develops under the most favourable conditions, we have a more or less complete democracy in the democratic republic. But this democracy is always hemmed in by the narrow limits set by capitalist exploitation, and consequently always remains, in effect, a democracy for the minority, only for the propertied classes, only for the rich. Freedom in capitalist society always remains about the same as it was in the ancient Greek republics: freedom for the slave-owners. Owing to the conditions of capitalist exploitation, the modern wage slaves are so crushed by want and poverty that 'they cannot be bothered with democracy', 'cannot be bothered with politics'; in the ordinary, peaceful course of events, the majority of the population is debarred from participation in public and political life.

The correctness of this statement is perhaps most clearly confirmed by Germany, because constitutional legality steadily endured there for a remarkably long time – nearly half a century (1871–1914) – and, during this period, the Social Democrats were able to achieve far more than in other countries in the way of 'utilizing legality', and organized a larger proportion of the workers into a political party than anywhere else in the world.

What is this largest proportion of politically conscious and active wage-slaves that has so far been recorded in capitalist society? One million members of the Social-Democratic Party – out of 15,000,000 wage-workers! Three million organized in trade unions – out of 15,000,000!

Democracy for an insignificant minority, democracy for the rich – that is the democracy of capitalist society. If we look more closely into the machinery of capitalist democracy, we see everywhere, in the 'petty' – supposedly petty – details of the suffrage (residential qualifications, exclusion of women, etc.), in the technique of the representative institutions, in the actual obstacles to the right of assembly (public buildings are not for 'paupers'!), in the purely capitalist organization of the daily press, etc., etc., – we see restriction after restriction upon democracy. These restrictions, exceptions, exclusions, obstacles for the poor seem slight, especially in the eyes of one who has never known want himself and has never been in close contact with the oppressed classes in their mass life (and nine out of ten, if not ninety-nine out of a hundred, bourgeois publicists and politicians come under this category); but, in their sum total, these restrictions exclude and squeeze out the poor from politics, from active participation in democracy.

Marx grasped this *essence* of capitalist democracy splendidly when, in analysing the experience of the Commune, he said that the oppressed are allowed once every few years to decide which particular representatives of the oppressing class shall represent and repress them in parliament!

But from this capitalist democracy – that is inevitably narrow and stealthily pushes aside the poor, and is therefore hypocritical and false through and through – forward development does not proceed simply, directly and smoothly, towards 'greater and greater democracy', as the liberal professors and petty-bourgeois opportunists would have us believe. No, forward development, i.e. development towards communism, proceeds through the dictatorship of the proletariat, and cannot do otherwise, for the *resistance* of the capitalist exploiters cannot be *broken* by anyone else or in any other way.

And the dictatorship of the proletariat – i.e. the organization of the vanguard of the oppressed as the ruling class for the purpose of suppressing the oppressors – cannot result merely in an expansion of democracy. *Simultaneously* with an immense expansion of democracy, which, *for the first time*, becomes democracy for the poor, democracy for the people, and not democracy for the money-bags, the dictatorship of the proletariat imposes a series of restrictions on the freedom of the oppressors, the exploiters, the capitalists. We must suppress them in order to free humanity from wage slavery, their resistance must be crushed by force; it is clear that there is no freedom and no democracy where there is suppression and where there is violence.

Engels expressed this splendidly in his letter to Bebel when he said, as the reader will remember, that 'the proletariat needs the state, not in the interests of freedom but in order to hold down its adversaries, and as soon as it becomes possible to speak of freedom the state as such ceases to exist'.

Democracy for the vast majority of the people, and suppression by force, i.e. exclusion from democracy, of the exploiters and oppressors of the people – this is the change democracy undergoes during the *transition* from capitalism to communism.

Only in communist society, when the resistance of the capitalists has disappeared, when there are no classes (i.e. when there is no distinction between the members of society as regards their relation to the social means of production), *only* then 'the state . . . ceases to exist', and *'it becomes possible to speak of freedom'*. Only then will a truly complete democracy become possible and be realized, a democracy without any exceptions whatever. And only then will democracy begin to *wither away*, owing to the simple fact that, freed from capitalist slavery, from the untold horrors, savagery, absurdities and infamies of capitalist exploitation, people will gradually *become accustomed* to observing the elementary rules of social intercourse that have been known for centuries and repeated for thousands of years in all copy-book maxims. They will become accustomed to observing them without force, without coercion, without subordination, *without the special apparatus* for coercion called the state.

The expression 'the state *withers away*' is very well chosen, for it indicates both the gradual and the spontaneous nature of the process. Only habit can, and undoubtedly will, have such an effect; for we see around us on millions of occasions how readily people become accustomed to observing the necessary rules of social intercourse when there is no exploitation, when there is nothing that arouses indignation, evokes protest and revolt, and creates the need for *suppression*.

And, so, in capitalist society, we have a democracy that is curtailed, wretched, false, a democracy only for the rich, for the minority. The dictatorship of the proletariat, the period of transition to communism, will, for the first time, create democracy for the people, for the majority, along with the necessary suppression of the exploiters, of the minority.

Communism alone is capable of providing really complete democracy, and the more complete it is, the sooner it will become unnecessary and wither away of its own accord.

In other words, under capitalism, we have the state in the proper sense of the word, that is, a special machine for the suppression of one class by another, and, what is more, of the majority by the minority. Naturally, to be successful, such an undertaking as the systematic suppression of the exploited majority by the exploiting minority calls for the utmost ferocity and savagery in the matter of suppressing, it calls for seas of blood, through which mankind is actually wading its way in slavery, serfdom and wage labour.

Furthermore, during the *transition* from capitalism to communism suppression is *still* necessary, but it is now the suppression of the exploiting minority by the exploited majority. A special apparatus, a special machine for suppression, the 'state', is *still* necessary, but this is now a transitional state. It is no longer a state in the proper sense of the word; for the suppression of the minority of exploiters by the majority of the wage slaves of *yesterday* is comparatively so easy, simple and natural a task that it will entail far less bloodshed than the suppression of the risings of slaves, serfs or wage-labourers, and it will cost mankind far less. And it is compatible with the extension of democracy to such an overwhelming majority of the population that the need for a *special machine* of suppression will begin to disappear. Naturally, the exploiters are unable to suppress the people without a highly complex machine for performing this task, but *the people* can suppress the exploiters even with a very simple 'machine', almost without a 'machine', without a special apparatus, by the simple *organization of the armed people* (such as the Soviets of Workers' and Soldiers' Deputies, we would remark, running ahead).

Lastly, only communism makes the state absolutely unnecessary, for there is *nobody* to be suppressed – 'nobody' in the sense of a *class*, of a systematic struggle against a definite section of the population. We are not utopians, and do not in the least deny the possibility and inevitability of excesses on the part of *individual persons*, or the need to stop *such* excesses. In the first place, however, no special machine, no special apparatus of suppression, is needed for this: this will be done by the armed people themselves, as simply and as readily as any crowd of civilized people, even in modern society, interferes to put a stop to a scuffle or to prevent a woman from being assaulted. And, second, we know that the fundamental social cause of excesses, which consist in the violation of the rules of social intercourse, is the exploitation of the people, their want and their poverty. With the removal of this chief cause, excesses will inevitably begin to *'wither away'*. We do not know how quickly and in what succession, but we do know they will wither away. With their withering away the state will also *wither away*.

Without building utopias, Marx defined more fully what can be defined *now* regarding this future, namely, the differences between the lower and higher phases (levels, stages) of communist society.

III. The First Phase of Communist Society

In the *Critique of the Gotha Programme*, Marx goes into detail to disprove Lassalle's idea that under socialism the worker will receive the 'undiminished' or 'full product of his labour'. Marx shows that from the whole of the social labour of society there must be deducted a reserve fund, a fund for the expansion of production, a fund for the replacement of the 'wear and tear' of machinery, and so on. Then, from the means of consumption must be deducted a fund for administrative expenses, for schools, hospitals, old people's homes, and so on.

Instead of Lassalle's hazy, obscure, general phrase ('the full product of his labour to the worker'), Marx makes a sober estimate of exactly how socialist society will have to manage its affairs. Marx proceeds to make a *concrete* analysis of the conditions of life of a society in which there will be no capitalism, and says:

> What we have to deal with here [in analysing the programme of the workers' party] is a communist society, not as it has *developed* on its own foundations, but, on the contrary, just as it *emerges* from capitalist society; which is thus in every respect, economically, morally, and intellectually, still stamped with the birthmarks of the old society from whose womb it comes.

It is this communist society, which has just emerged into the light of day out of the womb of capitalism and which is, in every respect, stamped with the birthmarks of the old society, that Marx terms the 'first', or lower, phase of communist society.

The means of production are no longer the private property of individuals. The means of production belong to the whole of society. Every member of society, performing a certain part of the socially necessary work, receives a certificate from society to the effect that they have done a certain amount of work. And, with this certificate, they receive from the public store of consumer goods a corresponding quantity of products. After a deduction is made of the amount of labour which goes to the public fund, every worker, therefore, receives from society as much as he has given to it.

'Equality' apparently reigns supreme.

But, when Lassalle, having in view such a social order (usually called socialism, but termed by Marx the first phase of communism), says that this is 'equitable distribution', that this is 'the equal right of all to an equal product of labour', Lassalle is mistaken and Marx exposes the mistake.

'Hence, the equal right,' says Marx, in this case *still* certainly conforms to 'bourgeois law', which, like all law, *implies inequality*. All law is an application of an *equal* measure to *different* people who in fact are not alike, are not equal to one another. That is why the 'equal right' is violation of equality and an injustice. In fact, everyone, having performed as much social labour as another, receives an equal share of the social product (after the above-mentioned deductions).

But people are not alike: one is strong, another is weak; one is married, another is not; one has more children, another has less, and so on. And the conclusion Marx draws is:

> With an equal performance of labour, and hence an equal share in the social consumption fund, one will in fact receive more than another, one will be richer than another, and so on. To avoid all these defects, the right instead of being equal would have to be unequal.

The first phase of communism, therefore, cannot yet provide justice and equality; differences, and unjust differences, in wealth will still persist, but the *exploitation* of man by man will have become impossible because it will be impossible to seize the *means of production* – the factories, machines, land, etc. – and make them private property. In smashing Lassalle's petty-bourgeois, vague phrases about 'equality' and 'justice' in general, Marx shows the *course of development* of communist society, which is *compelled* to abolish at first only the 'injustice' of the means of production seized by individuals, and which is *unable* at once to eliminate the other injustice, which consists in the distribution of consumer goods 'according to the amount of labour performed' (and not according to needs).

The vulgar economists, including the bourgeois professors and 'our' Tugan-Baranovsky,[2] constantly reproach the socialists with forgetting the inequality of people and with 'dreaming' of eliminating this inequality. Such a reproach, as we see, only proves the extreme ignorance of the bourgeois ideologists.

Marx not only most scrupulously takes account of the inevitable inequality of men, but he also takes into account the fact that the mere conversion of the means of production into the common property of the whole society (commonly called 'socialism') *does not remove* the defects of distribution and the inequality of 'bourgeois laws' which *continues to prevail* so long as products are divided 'according to the amount of labour performed'. Continuing, Marx says:

> But these defects are inevitable in the first phase of communist society as it is when it has just emerged, after prolonged birth pangs, from capitalist society. Law can never be higher than the economic structure of society and its cultural development conditioned thereby.

And so, in the first phase of communist society (usually called socialism) 'bourgeois law' is *not* abolished in its entirety, but only in part, only in proportion to the economic revolution so far attained, i.e. only in respect of the means of production. 'Bourgeois law' recognizes them as the private property of individuals. Socialism converts them into *common* property. *To that extent* – and to that extent alone – 'bourgeois law' disappears.

However, it persists as far as its other part is concerned; it persists in the capacity of regulator (determining factor) in the distribution of products and the allotment of labour among the members of society. The socialist principle, 'He who does not work shall not eat', is *already* realized; the other socialist principle, 'An equal amount of products for an equal amount of labour', is also *already* realized. But this is not yet communism, and it does not yet abolish 'bourgeois law', which gives unequal individuals, in return for unequal (really unequal) amounts of labour, equal amounts of products.

This is a 'defect', says Marx, but it is unavoidable in the first phase of communism; for if we are not to indulge in utopianism, we must not think that having overthrown capitalism people will at once learn to work for society *without any rules of law*. Besides, the abolition of capitalism *does not immediately create* the economic prerequisites for *such* a change.

Now, there are no other rules than those of 'bourgeois law'. To this extent, therefore, there still remains the need for a state, which, while safeguarding the common ownership of the means of production, would safeguard equality in labour and in the distribution of products.

The state withers away insofar as there are no longer any capitalists, any classes, and, consequently, no *class* can *be suppressed*.

But the state has not yet completely withered away, since there still remains the safeguarding of 'bourgeois law', which sanctifies actual inequality. For the state to wither away completely, complete communism is necessary.

IV. The Higher Phase of Communist Society

Marx continues:

> In a higher phase of communist society, after the enslaving subordination of the individual to the division of labour, and with it also the antithesis between mental and physical labour, has vanished, after labour has become not only a livelihood but life's prime want, after the productive forces have increased with the all-round development of the individual, and all the springs of co-operative wealth flow more abundantly – only then can the narrow horizon of bourgeois law be left behind in its entirety and society inscribe on its banners: From each according to his ability, to each according to his needs!

Only now can we fully appreciate the correctness of Engels's remarks mercilessly ridiculing the absurdity of combining the words 'freedom' and 'state'. So long as the state exists there is no freedom. When there is freedom, there will be no state.

The economic basis for the complete withering away of the state is such a high state of development of communism at which the antithesis between mental and physical labour disappears, at which there consequently disappears one of the principal sources of modern *social* inequality – a source, moreover, which cannot on any account be removed immediately by the mere conversion of the means of production into public property, by the mere expropriation of the capitalists.

This expropriation will make it *possible* for the productive forces to develop to a tremendous extent. And, when we see how incredibly capitalism is already *retarding* this development, when we see how much progress could be achieved on the basis of the level of technique already attained, we are entitled to say with the fullest confidence that the expropriation of the capitalists will inevitably result in an enormous development of the productive forces of human society. But how rapidly this development will proceed, how soon it will reach the point of breaking away from the division of labour, of doing away with the antithesis between mental and physical labour, of transforming labour into 'life's prime want' – we do not and *cannot* know.

That is why we are entitled to speak only of the inevitable withering away of the state, emphasizing the protracted nature of this process and its dependence upon the rapidity of development of the *higher phase* of communism, and leaving the question of the time required for, or the concrete forms of, the withering away quite open, because there is *no* material for answering these questions.

The state will be able to wither away completely when society adopts the rule: 'From each according to his ability, to each according to his needs', i.e. when people have become so accustomed to observing the fundamental rules of social intercourse and when their labour has become so productive that they will voluntarily work *according to their ability*. 'The narrow horizon of bourgeois law', which compels one to calculate with the heartlessness of a Shylock whether one has not worked half an hour more than anybody else – this narrow horizon will then be left behind. There will then be no need for society, in distributing the products, to regulate the quantity to be received by each; each will take freely 'according to his needs'.

From the bourgeois point of view, it is easy to declare that such a social order is 'sheer utopia' and to sneer at the socialists for promising everyone the right to receive from society, without any control over the labour of the individual citizen, any quantity of truffles, cars, pianos, etc. Even to this day, most bourgeois 'savants' confine themselves to sneering in this way, thereby betraying both their ignorance and their selfish defence of capitalism.

Ignorance – for it has never entered the head of any socialist to 'promise' that the higher phase of the development of communism will arrive; as for the greatest socialists' *forecast* that it will arrive, it presupposes not the present ordinary run of people, who, like the seminary students in Pomyalovsky's stories, are capable of damaging the stocks of public wealth 'just for fun', and of demanding the impossible.[3]

Until the 'higher' phase of communism arrives, the socialists demand the *strictest* control by society *and by the state* over the measure of labour and the measure of consumption; but this control must *start* with the expropriation of the capitalists, with the establishment of workers' control over the capitalists, and must be exercised not by a state of bureaucrats, but by a state of *armed workers*.

The selfish defence of capitalism by the bourgeois ideologists (and their hangers-on, like the Tseretelis, Chernovs and co.) consists in that they *substitute* arguing and talk about the distant future for the vital and burning question of *present-day* politics, namely, the expropriation of the capitalists, the conversion of *all* citizens into workers and other employees of *one* huge 'syndicate' – the whole state – and the complete subordination of the entire work of this syndicate to a genuinely democratic state, *the state of the Soviets of Workers' and Soldiers' Deputies.*

In fact, when a learned professor, followed by the philistine, followed in turn by the Tseretelis and Chernovs, talks of wild utopias, of the demagogic promises of the Bolsheviks, of the impossibility of 'introducing' socialism, it is the higher stage, or phase, of communism he has in mind, which no one has ever promised or even thought to 'introduce', because, generally speaking, it cannot be 'introduced'.

And this brings us to the question of the scientific distinction between socialism and communism which Engels touched on in his above-quoted argument about the incorrectness of the name 'Social Democrat'. Politically, the distinction between the first, or lower, and the higher phase of communism will in time, probably, be tremendous. But it would be ridiculous to recognize this distinction now, under capitalism, and only individual anarchists, perhaps, could invest it with primary importance (if there still are people among the anarchists who have learned nothing from the 'Plekhanov' conversion of the Kropotkins, of Grave, Corneliseen,[4] and other 'stars' of anarchism into social-chauvinists or 'anarchopatriots', as Ghe, one of the few anarchists who have still preserved a sense of humour and a conscience, has put it).[5]

But the scientific distinction between socialism and communism is clear. What is usually called socialism was termed by Marx the 'first', or lower, phase of communist society. Insofar as the means of production becomes *common* property, the word 'communism' is also applicable here, providing we do not forget that this is *not* complete communism. The great significance of Marx's explanations is that here, too, he consistently applies materialist dialectics, the theory of development, and regards communism as something which develops *out of* capitalism. Instead of scholastically invented, 'concocted' definitions and fruitless disputes over words (What is socialism? What is communism?), Marx gives an analysis of what might be called the stages of the economic maturity of communism.

In its first phase, or first stage, communism *cannot*, as yet, be fully mature economically and entirely free from traditions or vestiges of capitalism. Hence the interesting phenomenon that communism in its first phase retains 'the narrow horizon of *bourgeois* law'. Of course, bourgeois law with regard to the distribution of *consumer* goods inevitably presupposes the existence of the *bourgeois state*, for law is nothing without an apparatus capable of *enforcing* the observance of the rules of law.

It follows that, under communism, there remains for a time not only bourgeois law, but even the bourgeois state, without the bourgeoisie!

This may sound like a paradox or simply a dialectical conundrum of which Marxism is often accused by people who have not taken the slightest trouble to study its extraordinarily profound content.

But, in fact, remnants of the old, surviving in the new, confront us in life at every step, both in nature and in society. And Marx did not arbitrarily insert a scrap of 'bourgeois' law into communism, but indicated what is economically and politically inevitable in a society emerging *out of the womb* of capitalism.

Democracy means equality. The great significance of the proletariat's struggle for equality and of equality as a slogan will be clear if we correctly interpret it as meaning the abolition of *classes*. But democracy means only *formal* equality. And as soon as equality is achieved for all members of society *in relation to* ownership of the means of production, that is, equality of labour and wages, humanity will inevitably be confronted with the question of advancing further from formal equality to actual equality, i.e. to the operation of the rule 'from each according to his ability, to each according to his needs'. By what stages, by means of what practical measures humanity will proceed to this supreme aim we do not and cannot know. But it is important to realize how infinitely mendacious is the ordinary bourgeois conception of socialism as something lifeless, rigid, fixed once and for all, whereas, in reality, *only* socialism will be the beginning of a rapid, genuine, truly mass forward movement, embracing first the *majority* and then the whole of the population, in all spheres of public and private life.

Democracy is of enormous importance to the working class in its struggle against the capitalists for its emancipation. But democracy is by no means a boundary not to be overstepped; it is only one of the stages on the road from feudalism to capitalism, and from capitalism to communism.

Democracy is a form of the state, it represents, on the one hand, the organized, systematic use of force against persons; but, on the other hand, it signifies the formal recognition of equality of citizens, the equal right of all to determine the structure of, and to administer, the state. This, in turn, results in the fact that, at a certain stage in the development of democracy, it first welds together the class that wages a revolutionary struggle against capitalism – the proletariat, and enables it to crush, smash to atoms, wipe off the face of the earth the bourgeois, even the republican-bourgeois, state machine, the standing army, the police and the bureaucracy and to substitute for them a *more* democratic state machine, but a state machine nevertheless, in the shape of armed workers who proceed to form a militia involving the entire population.

Here, 'quantity turns into quality': *such* a degree of democracy implies overstepping the boundaries of bourgeois society and beginning its socialist reorganization. If really *all* take part in the administration of the state, capitalism cannot retain its hold. The development of capitalism, in turn, creates the *preconditions that enable* really 'all' to take part in the administration of the state. Some of these preconditions are: universal literacy, which has already been achieved in a number of the most advanced capitalist countries, then the 'training and disciplining' of millions of workers by the huge, complex, socialized apparatus of the postal service, railways, big factories, large-scale commerce, banking, etc., etc.

Given these *economic* preconditions, it is quite possible, after the overthrow of the capitalists and the bureaucrats, to proceed immediately, overnight, to replace them in the *control* over production and distribution, in the work of *keeping account* of labour and products, by the armed workers, by the whole of the armed population. (The question of control and accounting should not be confused with the question of the scientifically trained staff of engineers, agronomists, and so on. These gentlemen are working today in obedience to the wishes of the capitalists and will work even better tomorrow in obedience to the wishes of the armed workers.)

Accounting and control – that is *mainly* what is needed for the 'smooth working', for the proper functioning, of the *first phase* of communist society. *All* citizens are transformed into hired employees of the state, which consists of the armed workers. *All* citizens become employees and workers of a *single* countrywide state 'syndicate'. All that is required is that they should work equally, do their proper share of work, and get equal pay; the accounting and control necessary for this have been *simplified* by capitalism to the utmost and reduced to the extraordinarily simple operations – which any literate person can perform – of supervising and recording, knowledge of the four rules of arithmetic, and issuing appropriate receipts.[6]

When the *majority* of the people begin independently and everywhere to keep such accounts and exercise such control over the capitalists (now converted into employees) and over the intellectual gentry who preserve their capitalist habits, this control will really become universal, general and popular; and there will be no getting away from it, there will be 'nowhere to go'.

The whole of society will have become a single office and a single factory, with equality of labour and pay.

But this 'factory' discipline, which the proletariat, after defeating the capitalists, after overthrowing the exploiters, will extend to the whole of society, is by no means our ideal, or our ultimate goal. It is only a necessary *step* for thoroughly cleansing society of all the infamies and abominations of capitalist exploitation, *and for further* progress.

From the moment all members of society, or at least the vast majority, have learned to administer the state *themselves*, have taken this work into their own hands, have organized control over the insignificant capitalist minority, over the gentry who wish to preserve their capitalist habits and over the workers who have been thoroughly corrupted by capitalism – from this moment, the need for government of any kind begins to disappear altogether. The more complete the democracy, the nearer the moment when it becomes unnecessary. The more democratic the 'state' which consists of the armed workers, and which is 'no longer a state in the proper sense of the word', the more rapidly *every form* of state begins to wither away.

For, when *all* have learned to administer and actually to independently administer social production, independently keep accounts and exercise control over the parasites, the sons of the wealthy, the swindlers and other 'guardians of capitalist traditions', the escape from this popular accounting and control will inevitably become so incredibly difficult, such a rare exception, and will probably be accompanied by such swift and severe punishment (for the armed workers are practical people and not sentimental intellectuals, and they scarcely allow anyone to trifle with them), that the *necessity* of observing the simple, fundamental rules of the community will very soon become a *habit*.

Then the door will be thrown wide open for the transition from the first phase of communist society to its higher phase, and with it to the complete withering away of the state.

6

THE VULGARIZATION OF
MARXISM BY OPPORTUNISTS

The question of the relation of the state to the social revolution, and of the social revolution to the state, like the question of revolution generally, was given very little attention by the leading theoreticians and publicists of the Second International (1889–1914). But the most characteristic thing about the process of the gradual growth of opportunism that led to the collapse of the Second International in 1914 is the fact that, even when these people were squarely faced with this question, they *tried to evade* it or ignored it.

In general, it may be said that evasiveness over the question of the relation of the proletarian revolution to the state – an evasiveness which benefited and fostered opportunism – resulted in the *distortion* of Marxism and in its complete vulgarization.

To characterize this lamentable process, if only briefly, we shall take the most prominent theoreticians of Marxism: Plekhanov and Kautsky.

I. Plekhanov's Controversy with the Anarchists

Plekhanov wrote a special pamphlet on the relation of anarchism to socialism, entitled *Anarchism and Socialism*, which was published in German in 1894.

In treating this subject, Plekhanov contrived completely to evade the most urgent, burning and most politically essential issue in the struggle against anarchism, namely, the relation of the revolution to the state, and the question of the state in general! His pamphlet falls into two distinct parts: one of them is historical and literary, and contains valuable material on the history of the ideas of Stirner, Proudhon and others; the other is philistine, and contains a clumsy dissertation on the theme that an anarchist cannot be distinguished from a bandit.

It is a most amusing combination of subjects and most characteristic of Plekhanov's whole activity on the eve of the revolution and during the revolutionary period in Russia. In fact, in the years 1905 to 1917, Plekhanov revealed himself as a semi-doctrinaire and semi-philistine who, in politics, trailed in the wake of the bourgeoisie.

We have now seen how, in their controversy with the anarchists, Marx and Engels with the utmost thoroughness explained their views on the relation of revolution to the state. In 1891, in his foreword to Marx's *Critique of the Gotha Programme*, Engels wrote that 'we' – that is, Engels and Marx – 'were at that time, hardly two years after the Hague Congress of the [First] International, engaged in the most violent struggle against Bakunin and his anarchists.'[1]

The anarchists had tried to claim the Paris Commune as their 'own', so to say, as a collaboration of their doctrine; and they completely misunderstood its lessons and Marx's analysis of these lessons. Anarchism has given nothing even approximating true answers to the concrete political questions: Must the old state machine be *smashed*? And *what* should be put in its place?

But to speak of 'anarchism and socialism' while completely evading the question of the state, *and disregarding* the whole development of Marxism before and after the Commune, meant inevitably slipping into opportunism. For what opportunism needs most of all is that the two questions just mentioned should *not* be raised at all. That, *in itself*, is a victory for opportunism.

II. Kautsky's Controversy with the Opportunists

Undoubtedly, an immeasurably larger number of Kautsky's works have been translated into Russian than into any other language. It is not without reason that some German Social Democrats say in jest that Kautsky is read more in Russia than in Germany (let us say, in parenthesis, that this jest has a far deeper historical meaning than those who first made it suspect. The Russian workers, by making in 1905 an unusually great and unprecedented demand for the best works of the best Social-Democratic literature and editions of these works in quantities unheard of in other countries, rapidly transplanted, so to speak, the enormous experience of a neighbouring, more advanced country to the young soil of our proletarian movement).

Besides his popularization of Marxism, Kautsky is particularly known in our country for his controversy with the opportunists, with Bernstein at their head. One fact, however, is almost unknown, one which cannot be ignored if we set out to investigate how Kautsky drifted into the morass of unbelievably disgraceful confusion and defence of social-chauvinism during the supreme crisis of 1914–15. This fact is as follows: shortly before he came out against the most prominent representatives of opportunism in France (Millerand and Jaurès) and in Germany (Bernstein), Kautsky betrayed very considerable vacillation. The Marxist *Zarya*,[2] which was published in Stuttgart in 1901–2, and advocated revolutionary proletarian views, was forced to *enter into controversy* with Kautsky and describe as 'elastic' the half-hearted, evasive resolution, conciliatory towards the opportunists, that he proposed at the International Socialist Congress in Paris in 1900.[3] Kautsky's letters published in Germany reveal no less hesitancy on his part before he took the field against Bernstein.

Of immeasurably greater significance, however, is the fact that, in his very controversy with the opportunists, in his formulation of the question and his manner of treating it, we can now see, as we study the *history* of Kautsky's latest betrayal of Marxism, his systematic deviation towards opportunism precisely on the question of the state.

Let us take Kautsky's first important work against opportunism, *Bernstein and the Social-Democratic Programme*. Kautsky refutes Bernstein in detail, but here is a characteristic thing:

Bernstein, in his *Premises of Socialism*, of Herostratean fame, accuses Marxism of *'Blanquism'* (an accusation since repeated thousands of times by the opportunists and liberal bourgeoisie in Russia against the revolutionary Marxists, the Bolsheviks). In this connection Bernstein dwells particularly on Marx's *The Civil War in France*, and tries, quite unsuccessfully, as we have seen, to identify Marx's views on the lessons of the Commune with those of Proudhon. Bernstein pays particular attention to the conclusion which Marx emphasized in his 1872 preface to the *Communist Manifesto*, namely, that 'the working class cannot simply lay hold of the ready-made state machinery and wield it for its own purposes'.

This statement 'pleased' Bernstein so much that he used it no less than three times in his book, interpreting it in the most distorted, opportunist way.

As we have seen, Marx meant that the working class must *smash, break, shatter* (*Sprengung*, explosion – the expression used by Engels) the whole state machine. But, according to Bernstein, it would appear as though Marx in these words warned the working class against excessive revolutionary zeal when seizing power.

A cruder more hideous distortion of Marx's idea cannot be imagined.

How, then, did Kautsky proceed in his most detailed refutation of Bernsteinism?

He refrained from analysing the utter distortion of Marxism by opportunism on this point. He cited the above-quoted passage from Engels's preface to Marx's *Civil War* and said that, according to Marx, the working class cannot *simply* take over the *ready-made* state machinery, but that, generally speaking, it *can* take it over – and that was all. Kautsky did not say a word about the fact that Bernstein attributed to Marx the *very opposite* of Marx's real idea, that since 1852 Marx had formulated the task of the proletarian revolution as being to 'smash' the state machine.

The result was that the most essential distinction between Marxism and opportunism on the subject of the tasks of the proletarian revolution was slurred over by Kautsky!

We can quite safely leave the solution of the problems of the proletarian dictatorship of the future,' said Kautsky, writing *'against'* Bernstein (German edition, p. 172). This is not a polemic *against* Bernstein, but, in essence, a *concession* to him, a surrender to opportunism; for, at present, the opportunists ask nothing better than to 'quite safely leave to the future' all fundamental questions of the tasks of the proletarian revolution.

From 1852 to 1891, or for forty years, Marx and Engels taught the proletariat that it must smash the state machine. Yet, in 1899, Kautsky, confronted with the complete betrayal of Marxism by the opportunists on this point, fraudulently *substituted* for the question whether it is necessary to smash this machine the question for the concrete forms in which it is to be smashed, and then sought refuge behind the 'indisputable' (and barren) philistine truth that concrete forms cannot be known in advance!!

A gulf separates Marx and Kautsky over their attitude towards the proletarian party's task of training the working class for revolution.

Let us take the next, more mature, work by Kautsky, which was also largely devoted to a refutation of opportunist errors. It is his pamphlet, *The Social Revolution*. In this pamphlet, the author chose as his special theme the question of 'the proletarian revolution' and 'the proletarian regime'. He gave much that was exceedingly valuable, but he *avoided* the question of the state. Throughout the pamphlet the author speaks of the winning of state power – and no more; that is, he has chosen a formula which makes a concession to the opportunists, inasmuch as it *admits* the possibility of seizing power *without* destroying the state machine. The very thing which Marx in 1872 declared to be 'obsolete' in the programme of the *Communist Manifesto*, is *revived* by Kautsky in 1902.

A special section in the pamphlet is devoted to the 'forms and weapons of the social revolution'. Here, Kautsky speaks of the mass political strike, of civil war, and of the 'instruments of the might of the modern large state, its bureaucracy and the army'; but he does not say a word about what the Commune has already taught the workers. Evidently, it was not without reason that Engels issued a warning, particularly to the German socialists, against 'superstitious reverence' for the state.

Kautsky treats the matter as follows: the victorious prole-tariat 'will carry out the democratic programme', and he goes on to formulate its clauses. But he does not say a word about the new material provided in 1871 on the subject of the replacement of bourgeois democracy by proletarian democ-racy. Kautsky disposes of the question by using such 'impres-sive-sounding' banalities as:

> Still, it goes without saying that we shall not achieve supremacy under the present conditions. Revolution itself presupposes long and deep-going struggles, which, in themselves, will change our present political and social structure.

Undoubtedly, this 'goes without saying', just as the fact that horses eat oats or the Volga flows into the Caspian. Only it is a pity that an empty and bombastic phrase about 'deep-going' struggles is used to *avoid* a question of vital importance to the revolutionary proletariat, namely, *what* makes *its* revolution 'deep-going' in relation to the state, to democracy, as distinct from previous, non-proletarian revolutions.

By avoiding this question, Kautsky *in practice* makes a concession to opportunism on this most essential point, although *in words* he declares stern war against it and stresses the importance of the 'idea of revolution' (how much is this 'idea' worth when one is afraid to teach the workers the concrete lessons of revolution?), or says, 'revolutionary ideal-ism before everything else', or announces that the English workers are now 'hardly more than petty bourgeois'.

'The most varied form of enterprises – bureaucratic [??], trade unionist, co-operative, private . . . can exist side by side in socialist society,' Kautsky writes.

> There are, for example, enterprises which cannot do without a bureaucratic [??] organization, such as the railways. Here the democratic organization may take the following shape: the workers elect delegates who form a sort of parliament, which establishes the working regulations and supervises the management of the bureaucratic apparatus. The management of other countries may be transferred to the trade unions, and still others may become co-operative enterprises.

This argument is erroneous; it is a step backward compared with the explanations Marx and Engels gave in the 1870s, using the lessons of the Commune as an example.

As far as the supposedly necessary 'bureaucratic' organization is concerned, there is no difference whatever between a railway and any other enterprise in large-scale machine industry, any factory, large shop, or large-scale capitalist agricultural enterprise. The technique of all these enterprises makes absolutely imperative the strictest discipline, the utmost precision on the part of everyone in carrying out his allotted task, for otherwise the whole enterprise may come to a stop, or machinery or the finished product may be damaged. In all these enterprises the workers will, of course, 'elect delegates who will form a *sort of parliament*'.

The whole point, however, is that this 'sort of parliament' will *not* be a parliament in the sense of a bourgeois parliamentary institution. The whole point is that this 'sort of parliament' will not merely 'establish the working regulations and supervize the management of the bureaucratic apparatus,' as Kautsky, whose thinking does not go beyond the bounds of bourgeois parliamentarianism, imagines. In socialist society, the 'sort of parliament' consisting of workers' deputies will, of course, 'establish the working regulations and supervize the management' of the 'apparatus', *but* this apparatus will *not* be 'bureaucratic'. The workers, after winning political power, will smash the old bureaucratic apparatus, shatter it to its very foundations, and raze it to the ground; they will replace it by a new one, consisting of the very same workers and other employees, *against* whose transformation into bureaucrats will at once be taken which were specified in detail by Marx and Engels: (1) not only election, but also recall at any time; (2) pay not to exceed that of a workman; (3) immediate introduction of control by *all*, so that *all* may become 'bureaucrats' for a time and that, therefore, *nobody* may be able to become a 'bureaucrat'.

Kautsky has not reflected at all on Marx's words: 'The Commune was a working, not parliamentary, body, executive and legislative at the same time.'

Kautsky has not understood at all the difference between bourgeois parliamentarism, which combines democracy (*not for the people*) with bureaucracy (*against the people*), and proletarian democracy, which will take immediate steps to cut bureaucracy down to the roots, and which will be able to carry these measures through to the end, to the complete abolition of bureaucracy, to the introduction of complete democracy for the people.

Kautsky here displays the same old 'superstitious reverence' for the state, and 'superstitious belief' in bureaucracy.

Let us now pass to the last and best of Kautsky's works against the opportunists, his pamphlet *The Road to Power* (which, I believe, has not been published in Russian, for it appeared in 1909, when reaction was at its height in our country). This pamphlet is a big step forward, since it does not deal with the revolutionary programme in general, as with the pamphlet of 1899 against Bernstein, or with the tasks of the social revolution irrespective of the time of its occurrence, as with the 1902 pamphlet, *The Social Revolution*; it deals with the concrete conditions which compels us to recognize that the 'era of revolutions' is *setting in*.

The author explicitly points to the aggravation of class antagonisms in general and to imperialism, which plays a particularly important part in this respect. After the 'revolutionary period of 1789–1871' in Western Europe, he says, a similar period began in the East in 1905. A world war is approaching with menacing rapidity. 'It [the proletariat] can no longer talk of premature revolution.' 'We have entered a revolutionary period.' The 'revolutionary era is beginning'.

These statements are perfectly clear. This pamphlet of Kautsky's should serve as a measure of comparison of what the German Social Democrats *promised to be* before the imperialist war and the depth of degradation to which they, including Kautsky himself, sank when the war broke out. 'The present situation,' Kautsky wrote in the pamphlet under survey, 'is fraught with the danger that we [i.e. the German Social Democrats] may easily appear to be more "moderate" than we really are.' It turned out that, in reality, the German Social-Democratic Party was much more moderate and opportunist than it appeared to be!

It is all the more characteristic, therefore, that, although Kautsky so explicitly declared that the era of revolution had already begun, in the pamphlet which he himself said was devoted to an analysis of the '*political* revolution', he again completely avoided the question of the state.

These evasions of the question, these omissions and equivocations, inevitably added up to that complete swing-over to opportunism with which we shall now have to deal.

Kautsky, the German Social Democrats' spokesman, seems to have declared: I abide by revolutionary views (1899), I recognize, above all, the inevitability of the social revolution of the proletariat (1902), I recognize the advent of a new era of revolutions (1909). Still, I am going back on what Marx said as early as 1852, since the question of the tasks of the proletarian revolution in relation to the state is being raised (1912).

It was in this point-blank form that the question was put in Kautsky's controversy with Pannekoek.[4]

III. Kautsky's Controversy with Pannekoek

In opposing Kautsky, Pannekoek came out as one of the representatives of the 'left radical' trend which included Rosa Luxemburg, Karl Radek and others. Advocating revolutionary tactics, they were united in the conviction that Kautsky was going over to the 'Centre', which wavered in an unprincipled manner between Marxism and opportunism. This view was proved perfectly correct by the war, when this 'Centrist' (wrongly called Marxist) trend, or Kautskyism, revealed itself in all its repulsive wretchedness.

In an article touching on the question of the state, entitled 'Mass Action and Revolution' (*Die Neue Zeit*, 1912, Vol. XXX, 2), Pannekoek described Kautsky's attitude as one of 'passive radicalism', as 'a theory of inactive expectancy'. 'Kautsky refuses to see the process of revolution,' wrote Pannekoek (p. 616). In presenting the matter in this way, Pannekoek approached the subject which interests us, namely, the tasks of the proletarian revolution in relation to the state.

'The struggle of the proletariat,' he wrote,

is not merely a struggle against the bourgeoisie *for* state power, but a struggle *against* state power . . . The content of this [the proletarian] revolution is the destruction and dissolution

[*Auflosung*] of the instruments of power of the state with the aid of the instruments of power of the proletariat . . . The struggle will cease only when, as the result of it, the state organization is completely destroyed. The organization of the majority will then have demonstrated its superiority by destroying the organization of the ruling minority.

(pp. 544, 548)

The formulation in which Pannekoek presented his ideas suffers from serious defects. But its meaning is clear nonetheless, and it is interesting to note *how* Kautsky combated it.

'Up to now,' he wrote, 'the antithesis between the Social Democrats and the anarchists has been that the former wished to win the state power while the latter wished to destroy it. Pannekoek wants to do both' (p. 724). Although Pannekoek's exposition lacks precision and concreteness – not to speak of other shortcomings of his article which have no bearing on the present subject – Kautsky seized precisely on the point of *principle* raised by Pannekoek; and, on *this fundamental point* of *principle*, Kautsky completely abandoned the Marxist position and went over wholly to opportunism. His definition of the distinction between the Social Democrats and the anarchists is absolutely wrong; he completely vulgarizes and distorts Marxism.

The distinction between Marxists and the anarchists is this: (1) The former, while aiming at the complete abolition of the state, recognize that this aim can only be achieved after classes have been abolished by the socialist revolution, as the result of the establishment of socialism, which leads to the withering away of the state. The latter want to abolish the state completely overnight, not understanding the conditions under which the state can be abolished. (2) The former recognize that, after the proletariat has won political power, it must completely destroy the old state machine and replace it by a new one consisting of an organization of the armed workers, of the type of the Commune. The latter, while insisting on the destruction of the state machine, have a very vague idea of *what* the proletariat will put in its place and *how* it will use its revolutionary power. The anarchists even deny that the revolutionary proletariat should use the state power, they reject its revolutionary dictatorship. (3) The former demand that the proletariat be trained for revolution by utilizing the present state. The anarchists reject this.

In this controversy, it is not Kautsky but Pannekoek who represents Marxism, for it was Marx who taught that the proletariat cannot simply win state power in the sense that the old state apparatus passes into new hands, but must smash this apparatus, must break it and replace it by a new one.

Kautsky abandons Marxism for the opportunist camp, for this destruction of the state machine, which is utterly unacceptable to the opportunists, completely disappears from his argument, and he leaves a loophole for them in that 'conquest' may be interpreted as the simple acquisition of a majority.

To cover up his distortion of Marxism, Kautsky behaves like a doctrinaire: he puts forward a 'quotation' from Marx himself. In 1850, Marx wrote that a 'resolute centralization of power in the hands of the state authority' was necessary, and Kautsky triumphantly asks: does Pannekoek want to destroy 'centralism'?

This is simply a trick, like Bernstein's identification of the views of Marxism and Proudhonism on the subject of federalism as against centralism.

Kautsky's 'quotation' is neither here nor there. Centralism is possible with both the old and the new state machine. If the workers voluntarily unite their armed forces, this will be centralism, but it will be based on the 'complete destruction' of the centralized state apparatus – the standing army, the police and the bureaucracy. Kautsky acts like an outright swindler by evading the perfectly well-known arguments of Marx and Engels on the Commune and plucking out a quotation which has nothing to do with the point at issue.

'Perhaps he [Pannekoek],' Kautsky continues,

wants to abolish the state functions of the officials? But we cannot do without officials even in the party and trade unions, let alone in the state administration. And our programme does not demand the abolition of state officials, but that they be elected by the people . . . We are discussing here not the form the administrative apparatus of the 'future state' will assume, but whether our political struggle abolishes [literally dissolves – *auflost*] the state power *before we have captured it* [Kautsky's italics]. Which ministry with its officials could be abolished?

Then follows an enumeration of the ministries of education, justice, finance and war.

No, not one of the present ministries will be removed by our political struggle against the government . . . I repeat, in order to prevent misunderstanding: we are not discussing here the form the 'future state' will be given by the victorious Social Democrats, but how the present state is changed by our opposition.

(p. 725)

This is an obvious trick. Pannekoek raised the question of *revolution*. Both the title of his article and the passages quoted above clearly indicate this. By skipping to the question of 'opposition', Kautsky substitutes the opportunist for the revolutionary point of view. What he says means: at present we are an opposition; what we shall be after we have captured power, that we shall see. *Revolution has vanished!* And that is exactly what the opportunists wanted.

The point at issue is neither opposition nor political struggle in general, but *revolution*. Revolution consists in the proletariat *destroying* the 'administrative apparatus' and the *whole* state machine, replacing it by a new one, made up of the armed workers. Kautsky displays a 'superstitious reverence' for 'ministries'; but why can they not be replaced, say, by committees of specialists working under sovereign, all-powerful Soviets of Workers' and Soldiers' Deputies?

The point is not at all whether the 'ministries' will remain, or whether 'committees of specialists' or some other bodies will be set up; that is quite immaterial. The point is whether the old state machine (bound by thousands of threads to the bourgeoisie and permeated through and through with routine and inertia) shall remain, or be *destroyed* and replaced by a *new one*. Revolution consists not in the new class commanding, governing with the aid of the *old* state machine, but in this class smashing this machine and commanding, governing with the aid of a new machine. Kautsky slurs over this *basic* idea of Marxism, or he does not understand it at all.

His question about officials clearly shows that he does not understand the lessons of the Commune or the teachings of Marx. 'We cannot do without officials even in the party and the trade unions.'

We cannot do without officials *under capitalism*, under *the rule of the bourgeoisie*. The proletariat is oppressed, the working people are enslaved by capitalism. Under capitalism, democracy is restricted, cramped, curtailed, mutilated by all the conditions of wage slavery, and the poverty and misery of the people. This and this alone is the reason why the functionaries of our political organizations and trade unions are corrupted – or, rather, tend to be corrupted – by the conditions of capitalism and betray a tendency to become bureaucrats, i.e. privileged persons divorced from the people and standing *above* the people.

That is the *essence* of bureaucracy; and until the capitalists have been expropriated and the bourgeoisie overthrown, even proletarian functionaries will inevitably be 'bureaucratized' to a certain extent.

According to Kautsky, since elected functionaries will remain under socialism, so will officials, so will the bureaucracy! This is exactly where he is wrong. Marx, referring to the example of the Commune, showed that under socialism functionaries will cease to be 'bureaucrats', to be 'officials', they will cease to be so *in proportion* as — in addition to the principle of election of officials — the principle of recall at any time is *also* introduced, *as* salaries are reduced to the level of the wages of the average workman, and *as* parliamentary institutions are replaced by 'working bodies, executive and legislative at the same time'.

As a matter of fact, the whole of Kautsky's argument against Pannekoek, and particularly the former's wonderful point that we cannot do without officials even in our party and trade union organizations, is merely a repetition of Bernstein's old 'arguments' against Marxism in general. In his renegade book, *The Premises of Socialism*, Bernstein combats the ideas of 'primitive' democracy, combats what he calls 'doctrinaire democracy': binding mandates, unpaid officials, impotent central representative bodies, etc. To prove that this 'primitive' democracy is unsound, Bernstein refers to the experience of the British trade unions, as interpreted by the Webbs.[5] Seventy years of development 'in absolute free-dom', he says (German edition, p. 137), convinced the trade unions that primitive democracy was useless, and they replaced it by ordinary democracy, i.e. parliamentarism combined with bureaucracy.

In reality, the trade unions did not develop 'in absolute freedom' *but in absolute capitalist slavery*, under which, it goes without saying, a number of concessions to the prevailing evil, violence, falsehood, exclusion of the poor from the affairs of 'higher' administration, 'cannot be done without'. Under socialism much of 'primitive' democracy will inevitably be revived, since, for the first time in the history of civilized society the *mass* of population will rise to taking an *independent* part, not only in voting and elections, *but also in the everyday administration* of the state. Under socialism, *all* will govern in turn and will soon become accustomed to no one governing.

Marx's critico-analytical genius saw in the practical measures of the Commune the *turning-point* which the opportunists fear and do not want to recognize because of their cowardice, because they do not want to break irrevocably with the bourgeoisie, and which the anarchists do not want to see, either because they are in a hurry or because they do not understand at all the conditions of great social changes. 'We must not even think of destroying the old state machine; how can we do without ministries and officials,' argues the opportunist, who is completely saturated with philistinism and who, at bottom, not only does not believe in revolution, in the creative power of revolution, but lives in mortal dread of it (like our Mensheviks and Socialist-Revolutionaries).

'We must think *only* of destroying the old state machine; it is no use probing into the *concrete* lessons of earlier proletarian revolutions and analysing *what* to put in the place of what has been destroyed, and *how*,' argues the anarchist (the best of the anarchist, of course, and not those who, following the Kropotkins and co., trail behind the bourgeoisie). Consequently, the tactics of the anarchist become the tactics of *despair* instead of a ruthlessly bold revolutionary effort to solve concrete problems while taking into account the practical conditions of the mass movement.

Marx teaches us to avoid both errors; he teaches us to act with supreme boldness in destroying the entire old state machine, and, at the same time, he teaches us to put the question concretely: the Commune was able, in the space of a few weeks, to *start* building a *new*, proletarian state machine by introducing such-and-such measures to provide wider democracy and to uproot bureaucracy. Let us learn revolutionary boldness from the Communards; let us see in their practical measures the *outline* of really urgent and immediately possible measures, and then, *following this road*, we shall achieve the complete destruction of bureaucracy.

The possibility of this destruction is guaranteed by the fact that socialism will shorten the working day, will raise the *people* to a new life, will create such conditions for the *majority* of the population as will enable *everybody*, without exception, to perform 'state functions', and this will lead to the *complete withering away* of every form of state in general.

'Its object [the object of the mass strike]', Kautsky continues,

> cannot be to *destroy* the state power; its only object can be to make the government compliant on some specific question, or to replace a government hostile to the proletariat by one willing to meet it half-way [*entgegenkommende*] . . . But never, under no circumstances can it [that is, the proletarian victory over a hostile government] lead to the *destruction* of the state power; it can lead only to a certain *shifting* [*verschiebung*] of the balance of forces *within* the state power . . . The aim of our political struggle remains, as in the past, the conquest of state power by winning a majority in parliament and by raising parliament to the ranks of master of the government.
>
> (pp. 726, 727, 732)

This is nothing but the purest and most vulgar opportunism: repudiating revolution in deeds, while accepting it in words. Kautsky's thoughts go no further than a 'government . . . willing to meet the proletariat half-way' – a step backward to philistinism compared with 1847, when the *Communist Manifesto* proclaimed 'the organization of the proletariat as the ruling class'.

Kautsky will have to achieve his beloved 'unity' with the Scheidemanns, Plekhanovs, and Vanderveldes, all of whom agree to fight for a government 'willing to meet the proletariat half-way'.

We, however, shall break with these traitors to socialism, and we shall fight for the complete destruction of the old state machine, in order that the armed proletariat itself *may become the government*. These are two vastly different things.

Kautsky will have to enjoy the pleasant company of the Legiens and Davids, Plekhanovs, Potresovs,[6] Tseretelis and Chernovs, who are quite willing to work for the 'shifting of the balance of forces within the state power', for 'winning a majority in parliament' and 'raising parliament to the ranks of master of the government'. A most worthy object, which is wholly acceptable to the opportunists and which keeps everything within the bounds of the bourgeois parliamentary republic.

We, however, shall break with the opportunists; and the entire class-conscious proletariat will be with us in the fight – not to 'shift the balance of forces', but *to overthrow the bourgeoisie*, to *destroy* bourgeois parliamentarism, for a democratic republic after the type of the Commune, or a republic of Soviets of Workers' and Soldiers' Deputies, for the revolutionary dictatorship of the proletariat.

To the right of Kautsky in international socialism there are trends such as *Sozialistische Monatshefte* in Germany (Legien,

David, Kolb,[7] and many others, including the Scandinavian Stauning and Branting),[8] Jaurès's followers and Vandervelde in France and Belgium; Turati, Treves and other right-wingers of the Italian Party;[9] the Fabians and 'Independents' (the Independent Labour Party, which, in fact, has always been dependent on the Liberals) in Britain; and the like. All these gentry, who play a tremendous, very often a predominant role in the parliamentary work and the press of their parties, repudiate outright the dictatorship of the proletariat and pursue a policy of undisguised opportunism. In the eyes of these gentry, the 'dictatorship' of the proletariat 'contradicts' democracy!! There is really no essential distinction between them and the petty-bourgeois democrats.

Taking this circumstance into consideration, we are justified in drawing the conclusion that the Second International, that is, the overwhelming majority of its official representatives, has completely sunk into opportunism. The experience of the Commune has been not only ignored but distorted. Far from inculcating in the workers' minds the idea that the time is nearing when they must act to smash the old state machine, replace it by a new one, and in this way make their political rule the foundation for the socialist reorganization of society, they have actually preached to the masses the very opposite and have depicted the 'conquest of power' in a way that has left thousands of loopholes for opportunism.

The distortion and hushing up of the question of the relation of the proletarian revolution to the state could not but play an immense role at a time when states, which possess a military apparatus expanded as a consequence of imperialist rivalry, have become military monsters which are exterminating millions of people in order to settle the issue as to whether Britain or Germany – this or that finance capital – is to rule the world.[10]

POSTSCRIPT TO THE FIRST EDITION

This pamphlet was written in August and September 1917. I had already drawn up the plan for the next, the seventh chapter, 'The Experience of the Russian Revolutions of 1905 and 1917'. Apart from the title, however, I had no time to write a single line of the chapter; I was 'interrupted' by a political crisis – the eve of the October revolution of 1917. Such an 'interruption' can only be welcomed; but the writing of the second part of this pamphlet ('The Experience of the Russian Revolutions of 1905 and 1917') will probably have to be put off for a long time. It is more pleasant and useful to go through the 'experience of revolution' than to write about it.

The Author
Petrograd
30 November 1917

NOTES

Introduction

1. Text originally published in *Stato e rivoluzione. La dottrina marxista dello Stato e i compiti del proletariato nella rivoluzione*, Rome: Edizioni PGreco, Collana Filorosso, 2022.

Preface to the First Edition

1. Plekhanov, Georgi Valentinovich (1856–1918): One of the founders of the first Marxist organization in Russia: the Emancipation of Labour group. Plekhanov had at one time been a member of the People's Will (*Narodnaya volya*). After the dissolution of the Emancipation of Labour group, Plekhanov later joined the Russian Social-Democratic party, becoming a Menshevik after the split in the party. During World War I, Plekhanov took what Lenin dubbed a social-chauvinist stance: that German victory would be disastrous for the world's proletariat, but an Entente victory would be much better for the world's proletariat. Plekhanov supported the World War, while millions of Russians were dying and refusing to fight, up until the Soviet government signed the treaty of Brest-Litovsk, which horrified Plekhanov. By the 1917 February Revolution, Plekhanov returned to Russia and gave his support to the provisional government, claiming it to have established a truly bourgeois government. By the time of the October Revolution, Plekhanov was outraged, and fought to usurp the Soviet government, believing it premature.

Breshkovskaya, Catherine (1844–1943): Russian revolutionary. Exiled to

Siberia for her political beliefs for much of her adult life. After being released she soon left the Russian Soviet Federative Socialist Republic (RSFSR), as a result of her opposition to the government.

Rubanovich, Ilya Adolfovich (1859–1920): Russian revolutionary who joined the People's Will in the 1880s. In 1881, this group assassinated Tsar Aleksandr II. During the repression which followed, Rubanovich fled abroad, eventually settling in Paris, France, and becoming a French citizen. There he co-founded the Group of Old Members of The People's Will (*Gruppa starykh narodovol'tsev*) in 1891, together with P. L. Lavrov, N. S. Rusanov and others. In 1900 he was instrumental in founding the Agrarian Socialist League. When the Socialist-Revolutionary Party (PSR) was founded in 1901, Rubanovich joined it and became its official representative abroad. Together with Nikolai Rusanov, he edited the party's official journal, *Herald of the Russian Revolution* (Vestnik russkoi revoliutsii). In 1914, most European socialist parties split over the First World War. Rubanovich sided with the 'Defencist' wing of the Russian PSR and the 'social patriots' in the SFIO, who supported the Entente war effort. Rubanovich supported the February Revolution of 1917, briefly returned to Russia and then returned to Paris to resume his position as representative of the PSR abroad. He opposed the October Revolution.

Hyndman, Henry Mayers (1842–1922): English Social Democrat. Up to 1880, when he got to know Marx, Hyndman was a democrat of an indefinite type who had connections and sympathies with the Tories. 'He achieved his turn to socialism after reading *Capital* (in the French translation) during one of the numerous voyages he made to America between 1874 and 1880.' (Lenin.) Founded the Social-Democratic Federation in 1881, which helped influence Australian Socialists, though it never became a mass organization. In 1914 he was an ardent patriot; after the October Revolution in Russia he was a supporter of intervention. Fabians – members of the Fabian Society, a British reformist organization founded in 1884. It grouped mostly bourgeois intellectuals – scholars, writers, politicians – including Sydney and Beatrice Webb, Ramsay MacDonald and Bernard Shaw. The Fabians denied the necessity for the proletarian class struggle and for the socialist revolution. They contended that the transition from capitalism to socialism could only be effected through minor social reforms, that is, gradual changes.

2. Karl Kautsky (1854–1938): German Social-Democratic theorist and editor of the party's journal *Die Neue Zeit*. At the prime of his career, Kautsky wrote such Marxist works as *The Economic Teachings of Karl Marx* (1886) and *The Agrarian Question* (1898). In the Second International, Kautsky took a centrist position between the Bernsteinians and the Left Social Democrats – F. Mehring, R. Luxemburg and K. Liebknecht. Kautsky supported Martov and the Mensheviks in their struggle against the Bolsheviks. On the question

of the dictatorship of the proletariat, he denied the need to destroy the bour-geois state machine. On the national-colonial question, Kautsky supported the positions of the right-wing Social Democrats, Russian Mensheviks, and Bundists. Lenin polemicized against Kautsky's theory of 'ultra-imperialism'. After the October Revolution, Kautsky helped the right-wing German Social Democrats stifle the German revolution of 1918–19 and opposed the strength-ening of ties with Soviet Russia.

1. Class Society of the State

1. See Frederick Engels, *The Origin of the Family, Private Property and the State* (Karl Marx and Frederick Engels, *Selected Works*, Vol. 3, Moscow, 1973, pp. 326–7). Further below, Lenin is quoting from the same work by Engels (Marx and Engels, *Selected Works*, Vol. 3, pp. 327–30).

2. Socialist-Revolutionary Party: The Socialist-Revolutionary Party, also known as Party of Socialist-Revolutionaries or Social Revolutionary Party (the SRs), was a major political party in late Imperial Russia, during both the February and October Revolutions, and in early Soviet Russia. The SRs were the ideological heirs of the Narodniks, agrarian socialists and support-ers of a democratic socialist Russian republic. The SRs won a mass following among the Russian peasantry by endorsing the overthrow of the Tsar and land redistribution. Controversially, the party leadership endorsed the Russian Provisional Government and participated in multiple coalitions with liberal and social-democratic parties, while a radical faction within the SRs rejected the provisional government's authority in favor of the Congress of Soviets and began to drift towards the Bolsheviks. These divisions would ultimately result in the party splitting over the course of the summer of 1917 into the Right and Left SRs.

Menshevik Party: Meaning 'minority' in Russian, the party was formed in 1903 from a split in the The Russian Social Democratic Labour Party (R.S.D.L.P), which created the Bolsheviki and Mensheviki parties. The Mensheviks believed that socialism should only be achieved firstly through a bourgeois revolution; following this revolution, they felt the working class and peasantry would then be able to revolt against the bourgeois, and estab-lish socialism. After the revolution of February 1917, most Mensheviks joined the provisional government, strongly subscribing to the theory of stagism. After the October Revolution the Mensheviks opposed the Soviet government, primarily through bureaucratic lobbying, though some members later joined the White armies.

3. Gentile, or tribal, organization of society – the primitive communal system, or the first socio-economic formation in history. The tribal commune

Notes for page 12

was a community of blood relatives linked by economic and social ties. The tribal system went through the matriarchal and the patriarchal periods. The patriarchate culminated in primitive society becoming a class society and in the rise of the state. Relations of production under the primitive communal system were based on social ownership of the means of production and equalitarian distribution of all products. This corresponded in the main to the low level of the productive forces and to their character at the time.

For the primitive communal system, see Karl Marx, 'Conspectus of Lewis Morgan's *Ancient Society*', and Frederick Engels, 'The Origin of the Family, Private Property and the State' (Marx and Engels, *Selected Works*, Vol. 3, pp. 204–334).

4. P. I. Palchinsky, Deputy Minister of Trade and Industry in the Kerensky Government in the summer of 1917, was one of the organizers of subversive acts engineered by capitalists who aimed at throttling the revolution by 'the bony hand of famine'.

5. Chernov, Victor Mikhailovich (1876–1952): One of the leaders and theoreticians of the Socialist-Revolutionaries. Entered politics in the early 1890s. Founder and leader of Russian Socialist-Revolutionary Party. Emigre 1899–1917. Participated in the Zimmerwald Anti-war Conference. Minister of Agriculture in Provisional Government from May–September 1917, a position in which he sanctioned repression against peasants who seized landed estates. Later elected Russian president. Chairman of the Constituent Assembly in 1918. Helped anti-Soviet risings by counter-revolutionary Czechoslovaks. Headed Ufa Directorate. Arrested by Kolchak and released. Emigrated to the West in 1920. Member of the Executive Committee of Second International.

Tsereteli, Irakly (1882–1959): Georgian Social Democrat. Member of the Second Duma. Exiled to Siberia by Tsar. Menshevik leader. A Centrist during WWI. A member of the Executive Committee of Petrograd Soviet 1917, Tsereteli became the first Minister of Posts and Telegraphs in the provisional government. After the July events he became Minister of the Interior, replacing Prince Lvov. After the October Revolution Tsereteli lead the anti-Soviet bloc in the Constituent Assembly which refused to recognize the Soviet government. Executive Committee member of the Second International. During the Civil War Tsereteli helped establish the Menshevik government of Georgia. After Stalin led the Red Army to invade Georgia (what became known as the Georgian Incident), the Menshevik government was overthrown and Tserteli thereafter lived in exile.

Avksentev, Nikolai (1878–1943): Old and leading right-wing member of the Socialist-Revolutionary Party. Member of 1905 Soviet and Executive Committee. A chauvinist in the War. Minister of Internal Affairs under Kerensky, August–September 1917. During the 1917 Revolution, Chairman,

All Russian Soviet of Peasants' Deputies of the Democratic Conference and the 'Preparliament' (Council of the Rebublic). On Ufa Directorate, expelled from Siberia by Whites. Emigrated 1919.

Skobelev, Matvei Ivanovich (1885–1937): Menshevik. Member of the fourth Duma. Vice-President Petrograd Soviet and member of Executive Committee. During the First World War Skobelev was a social-chauvinist. In 1917 he became Minister of Labour in the second (April) provisional government. Joined the Communist Party in 1922.

6. See Frederick Engels, *Anti-Dühring*, Moscow, 1969, pp. 332–3. Further down, Lenin quotes from the same work by Engels (*Anti-Duhring*, p. 220).

7. See Karl Marx, *The Poverty of Philosophy*, Moscow, 1973, pp. 151–2.

8. See Marx and Engels, *Selected Works*, Vol. 1, p. 137.

9. Gotha Programme – the programme adopted by the Socialist Workers' Party of Germany in 1875, at the Gotha Congress, which united two German socialist parties, namely, the Eisenachers – led by August Bebel and Wilhelm Liebknecht and influenced by Marx and Engels – and the Lassalleans. The programme betrayed eclecticism and was opportunist, because the Eisenachers had made concessions to the Lassalleans on major issues and accepted Lassallean formulations. Marx in his *Critique of the Gotha Programme*, and Engels in his letter to Bebel of 18–28 March 1875, devastated the Gotha Programme, which they regarded as a serious step backwards compared with the Eisenach programme of 1869.

2. The Experience of 1848–51

1. See Marx, *Poverty of Philosophy*, p. 151.

2. See Marx and Engels, *Selected Works*, Vol. 1, pp. 118–19 and 126.

3. See Karl Marx, *The Eighteenth Brumaire of Louis Bonaparte* (Marx and Engels, *Selected Works*, Vol. I, p. 477). Further below, Lenin is quoting from Engels's preface to the third edition of the work (*Eighteenth Brumaire*, p. 396).

4. Cadets (Constitutional Democrats): A Russian party formed in October 1905, called Cadets from its abbreviated name for members of the Constitutional-Democratic Party, and also known as the 'Party of the People's Freedom'.

The Cadets were social-chauvinists during the First World War. The Cadet party were reformists who sought to retain the monarchy but establish parliamentry rule over Russia. During the February Revolution of 1917, the Cadets made several attempts to save the monarchy but failed. They later formed the strongest party of the provisional government. The Cadet Ministry, however, was overthrown in April because it declared itself in favour of the World War, including the imperialistic aims of expanding

Russia's borders. After the October Revolution of 1917, the Cadets assisted the French, US, Japanese and British invading armies to overthrow the RSFSR. After the defeat of the White armies in 1922, the Cadets moved overseas; some of its members continued to assist the Imperialists with usurping the Soviet government.

5. Mehring, Franz (1846–1919): Became German radical democrat in 1870s, sympathetic to Lassalleanism; won to Marxism and joined SPD 1891; chief editor of *Leipziger Volkszeitung* 1902–7; a leading contributor to Die Neue Zeit; author of *History of German Social-Democracy* and biography of Marx; close collaborator of Rosa Luxemburg from 1912; founding member of Spartacus current 1914–15, and CP 1918.

6. *Die Neue Zeit* – theoretical journal of the German Social-Democratic Party, published in Stuttgart from 1883 to 1923. It was edited by Karl Kautsky till October 1917 and by Heinrich Cunow in the subsequent period. It published some of Marx's and Engels's writings for the first time. Engels offered advice to its editors and often criticized them for departures from Marxism.

In the second half of the 1890s, upon Engels's death, the journal began systematically to publish revisionist articles, including a serial by Bernstein entitled 'Problems of Socialism', which initiated a revisionist campaign against Marxism. During the First World War the journal adhered to a Centrist position, and virtually backed the social-chauvinists.

7. Weydemeyer, Joseph (1818–66): Prussian artillery officer. Writer. At first a supporter of 'true socialism', he became, in 1845–46, a follower of Marx and Engels. Member of the League of Communists; in 1849–51, head of its Frankfurt chapter. He visited Marx in Brussels, stayed there for a time and attended Marx's lectures. Participated in the 1848 Revolution. One of the 'responsible editors' of the *Neue Rheinische Zeitung* in 1849–50. There too he wrote out large parts of the manuscript of the *Deutsche Ideologie* (German Ideology) in a fair copy. Collaborated in socialist periodicals: the *Westphälisches Dampfboot* (Westphalian Steamboat) and the *Neue Rheinische Zeitung*. In 1851 he emigrated from Germany to America and worked there as a journalist. He took part in the war against the Southern slave owners as colonel of a regiment in the Union Army.

8. See Karl Marx and Frederick Engels, *Selected Correspondence*, Moscow, 1965.

3. Experience of the Paris Commune of 1871: Marx's Analysis

1. See Marx and Engels, *Selected Works*, Vol. 1, p. 22.

2. Kugelman, Ludwig (1830–1902): German socialist and doctor. Friend and correspondent of Karl Marx. Member of the First International.

3. See Marx and Engels, *Selected Correspondence*, pp. 262–3. (The letters of Marx to Kugelmann have appeared in Russian in no less than two editions, one of which I edited and supplied with a preface.) – *Lenin*

4. All the following quotes in this chapter, with one exception, are so cited.

5. See Karl Marx, *The Civil War in France* (Marx and Engels, *Selected Works*, Vol. 2, pp. 217–21). Further below, Lenin is quoting from the same work by Marx (Marx and Engels, *Selected Works*, Vol. 2, pp. 222, 220–3).

6. Bernstein, Eduard (1850–1932): German socialist; collaborator of Engels; theorist of revisionist current in SPD from 1898; member of USPD during War; opponent of Comintern; rejoined SPD in 1919; Reichstag deputy 1902–7, 1912–18, 1920–8.

7. Scheidemann, Philipp (1865–1939): Joined German Social Democracy in 1883; member SPD executive 1911; co-chair of Reichstag fraction 1913; social-chauvinist during War; led in suppressing workers' revolution 1918–19; German prime minister February to June 1919; forced by Nazis into emigration 1933.

David, Eduard (1863–1930): Right-wing German social democrat. Supported WWI. Minister in Ebert Cabinet 1919–20. President of National Assembly, 1919.

Legien, Carl (1861–1920): Joined SPD 1885; chairman of lathe operators' union 1887 and of confederation of pro-socialist unions 1890; member of Reichstag from 1893; supported government war effort 1914–18 and SPD right-wing majority; as chairman of main German union federation, called general strike that defeated Kapp Putsch 1920.

Sembat, Marcel (1862–1922): Elected French socialist deputy 1893, becoming leading figure in parliamentary group; member of SP National Council from 1905; supported French war effort, becoming minister of public works 1914–16; opposed SP affiliation to Comintern and remained in Dissident party after 1920 split.

Renaudel, Pierre (1871–1935): The leader of the French Socialist Party following Jaurès's assassination. From 1914 he was a member of the Chamber of Deputies. During the First World War he took a defencist position. In 1920, after the split in the French Socialist Party at the Tours Congress, he remained leader of the minority which refused to affiliate with the Comintern. He subsequently headed the right wing of the party standing for unification with the radical socialists.

Henderson, Arthur (1863–1935): Iron moulder; organizer for British Iron Founders' union 1892; as union leader, favoured moderate course and avoidance of strikes; member of Labour Party from its formation and of its right wing; three times party leader; social-chauvinist during War; cabinet member 1924 and 1929–31.

Vandervelde, Émile (1866–1938): Leader of Belgian Workers' Party; chairman of Brussels office of Second International 1900–14; member of Belgian council of ministers 1916–21, 1925–7, 1936–7; chairman of Belgian Workers' Party 1933–8; president of Socialist International 1929–36.

Thorvald August Marinus Stauning (1873–1942): Was the first social-democratic prime minister of Denmark. He served as prime minister from 1924 to 1926 and again from 1929 until his death in 1942.

Branting, Hjalmar (1860–1925): Wrested control of the Social-Demokraten editorship from August Palm and took Swedish Social Democracy in a reformist direction. Prime Minister of Sweden, serving for three separate periods in 1920, 1922–23, and 1924–25. Awarded Nobel Peace Prize in 1921.

Bissolati, Leonida (1857–1920): Founding member of Italian SP 1892; editor of *Avanti* 1896–1903, 1908–10; saw British Labour Party as model; expelled from SP 1912 for supporting Italy's war in Libya; founded Reformist Socialist Party, which supported Italy's entry into war; government minister 1916–18.

8. Rusanov, Nikolay Sergeyevich (1859–1939): Also known under the pseudonyms of K. Tarasov and N. Kudrin, he was a Russian revolutionary who connected the revolutionary populist movement of the 1870s with the revolutionary parties of the early twentieth century, particularly the Russian Socialist-Revolutionary Party (PSR). After the February Revolution of 1917, Rusanov supported the provisional government and A. F. Kerensky. He opposed the Bolshevik October Revolution and in 1918 emigrated to Western Europe. At first he settled in Berlin, but eventually he moved to Bern, Switzerland, where he died in 1939. He wrote his memoirs in two parts, published under the titles *In Emigration* (1929) and *In the Homeland* (1931).

Zenzinov, Vladimir Mikhailovich (1880–1953): A member of Russia's Socialist-Revolutionary Party, a participant of the First (1905), Second (February 1917), and Third (October 1917) Russian Revolutions, and an author of several books. Zenzinov opposed the October Revolution. He was elected as an SR deputy to the Constituent Assembly, dissolved by the Bolsheviks in 1918. Thereafter Zenzinov joined the rump Constituent Assembly government in Samara in 1918. He was briefly one of the Directors of the Provisional All-Russian Government, together with N. D. Avksentiev and others. Zenzinov was exiled to China after being arrested during a military coup by Admiral Kolchak in November 1918. From there he made his way back to Western Europe. He lived in Berlin until Hitler came to power in 1933, after which he relocated to Paris. During this time he published several more books and worked for a variety of émigré socialist journals, including *Volya Rossiya*, *Golos Rossii*, *Dni*, *Novaya Rossiya* and *Sovremennye zapiski*. In 1939, Zenzinov went to Finland to witness the beginning of World War II and the

Soviet attack on Finland, and to gather information on Russia. In 1940, Zenzinov emigrated to the United States, settling in New York and writing his memoirs.

9. The Girondists – a political grouping during the French bourgeois revolution of the late eighteenth century, expressed the interests of the moderate bourgeoisie. They wavered between revolution and counter-revolution, and made deals with the monarchy.

4. Supplementary Explanations by Engels

1. See Frederick Engels, *The Housing Question* (Marx and Engels, *Selected Works*, Vol. 2, pp. 317–18). Further below, Lenin is quoting from the same work by Engels (Marx and Engels, *Selected Works*, Vol. 2, pp. 370, 355).

2. Lenin is referring to the articles "L'indifferenza in materia politica" by Karl Marx and "Dell' Autorita" by Frederick Engels (*Almanacco Republicano per l'anno* 1874). Further below, Lenin is quoting from the same articles.

3. Bebel, August (1840–1913): Turner; a founder of German socialist movement; collaborator of Marx and Engels; central leader of SPD from its foundation until his death; author of *Women and Socialism*; opposed revisionism in SPD but eventually moved toward centrist positions.

4. Bracke, Hermann August Franz Wilhelm Gotthard (1842–80): Social-democratic publisher and journalist. He participated in the foundation of the German Social-Democratic Workers' Party (SPAD) which later became the SPD.

5. See Marx and Engels, *Selected Correspondence*, pp. 293–4.

6. Bakunin, Mikhail (1814–76): Russian anarchist; leader of split with Marxist forces in First International.

7. Erfurt Programme – the programme adopted by the German Social-Democratic Party at its Erfurt Congress in October 1891. A step forward compared with the Gotha Programme (1875), it was based on Marx's doctrine of the inevitable downfall of the capitalist mode of production and its replacement by the socialist mode. It stressed the necessity for the working class to wage a political struggle, pointed out the party's role as the leader of that struggle, and so on. But it also made serious concessions to opportunism. Engels criticized the original draft of the programme in detail in his work *A Critique of the Draft Social-Democratic Programme of 1891*. It was virtually a critique of the opportunism of the Second International as a whole. But the German Social-Democratic leaders concealed Engels's critique from the rank and file, and disregarded his highly important comments in drawing up the final text of the programme.

8. Liebknecht, Wilhelm (1826–1900): Participant in 1848 revolution in

Germany; collaborator of Marx and Engels; co-founder of German Social Democracy 1869 and, with Bebel, leader of SPD until his death; chief editor of *Vorwärts* 1876–8, 1891–1900.

9. The Anti-Socialist Law (Exceptional Law Against the Socialists) was enacted in Germany by the Bismarck government in 1878 to combat the working-class and socialist movement. Under this law, all Social-Democratic Party organizations, all mass organizations of the workers, and the working-class press were banned, socialist literature was confiscated and the Social Democrats were persecuted, to the point of banishment. These repressive measures did not, however, break the Social-Democratic Party, which readjusted itself to illegal conditions. *Der Soʒial-Demokrat*, the party's central organ, was published abroad and party congresses were held at regular intervals (1880, 1883 and 1887). In Germany herself, the Social-Democratic organizations and groups were coming back to life underground, an illegal Central Committee leading their activities. Besides, the Party widely used legal opportunities to establish closer links with the working people, and its influence was growing steadily. At the Reichstag elections in 1890, it polled three times as many votes as in 1878. Marx and Engels did much to help the Social Democrats. In 1890, popular pressure and the growing working-class movement led to the annulment of the Anti-Socialist Law.

10. See Marx and Engels, *Selected Works*, Vol. 2, pp. 178–89. Further below, Lenin is quoting from the same work (*Selected Works*, Vol. 2, pp. 179–80, 184, 187–9).

11. Cavaignac, Louis-Eugène (1802–57): A French general and politician who served as chief executive of France between June and December 1848, during the French Second Republic. As Minister of War in the French provisional government, Cavaignac was temporarily given emergency powers to put down the June Days uprising, a revolt by Parisian workers against the National Assembly. After suppressing the insurrection he renounced his dictatorial powers, and was subsequently confirmed by the National Assembly as the provisional 'Chief of the Executive Power' of France, governing for nearly six months until the 1848 presidential election, in which he ran but lost to Louis-Napoléon Bonaparte. He continued to serve as a representative in the National Assembly until its dissolution by the president during the 1851 coup d'état, and afterwards retired.

12. The Los-von-Kirche-Bewegung (the Leave-the-Church movement), or Kirchenaustrittsbewegung (Movement to Secede from the Church) assumed a vast scale in Germany before the First World War. In January 1914, *Die Neue Zeit* began, with the revisionist Paul Göhre's article 'Kirchenaustrittsbewegung und Sozialdemokratie' ('The Movement to Secede from the Church and Social Democracy'), to discuss the attitude of

the German Social-Democratic Party to the movement. During that discussion prominent German Social-Democratic leaders failed to rebuff Göhre, who affirmed that the party should remain neutral towards the Movement to Secede from the Church and forbid its members to engage in propaganda against religion and the Church on behalf of the party.

Lenin took notice of the discussion while working on material for *Imperialism, the Highest Stage of Capitalism*.

13. Lassalleans – supporters of the German socialist Ferdinand Lassalle, members of the General Association of German Workers founded at the Congress of Workers' Organizations, held in Leipzig in 1863, to counterbalance the bourgeois progressists who were trying to gain influence over the working class. The first president of the association was Lassalle, who formulated its programme and the fundamentals of its tactics. The association's political programme was declared to be the struggle for universal suffrage, and its economic programme, the struggle for workers' production associations, to be subsidized by the state. In their practical activities, Lassalle and his followers adapted themselves to the hegemony of Prussia and supported the Great Power policy of Bismarck. 'Objectively,' wrote Engels to Marx on 27 January 1865, 'this was a base action and a betrayal of the whole working-class movement to the Prussians.' Marx and Engels frequently and sharply criticized the theory, tactics and organizational principles of the Lassalleans as an opportunist trend in the German working-class movement.

14. See Frederick Engels, 'Vorwort zur Broschüre Internationales aus dem "Volksstaat" (1871–1875)', in Marx-Engels, *Werke*, Bd. 22, Berlin, 1963, pp. 417–18.

5. The Economic Basis of the Withering Away of the State

1. See Karl Marx, *Critique of the Gotha Programme* (Marx and Engels, *Selected Works*, Vol. 3, p. 26). Further below, Lenin is quoting from the same work by Marx (Marx and Engels, *Selected Works*, Vol. 3, pp. 26, 17, 19).

2. Tugan-Baranovsky, Mikhail (1865–1919): Ukrainian economist; contributor to Marxist theory of crises; joined liberal bourgeois Cadet party during 1905–7 revolution; active in cooperative movement; opponent of Russian October revolution; minister of Ukrainian People's Republic 1917–18.

3. The reference is to the pupils of a seminary who won notoriety by their extreme ignorance and barbarous customs. They were portrayed by N. G. Pomyalovsky, a Russian author.

4. Kropotkin, Peter (1842–1921): Russian anarchist, writer and geographer. Opposed to the Bolsheviks, spent most of his life outside Russia, but returned before his death.

Grave, Jean (1854–1939): An important activist in the French anarchist and the international anarchist communism movements. He was the editor of three major anarchist periodicals, *Le Révolté*, *La Révolte* and *Les Temps Nouveaux*, and wrote dozens of pamphlets and a number of important anarchist books. In 1914 Grave joined Kropotkin in England, and incurred the wrath of anti-war anarchists by signing the *Manifesto of the Sixteen*, which supported the allies during World War I.

Cornelissen, Christiaan Gerardus (1864–1942): A Dutch syndicalist writer, economist, and trade unionist.

5. The 'Ghe' referred to here is actually Aleksandr Yulievich Ge.

6. When the more important functions of the state are reduced to such accounting and control by the workers themselves, it will cease to be a 'political state' and 'public functions will lose their political character and become mere administrative functions' (*cf.* above, Chapter 4, II, Engels's controversy with the anarchists). – *Lenin*

6. The Vulgarization of Marxism by Opportunists

1. The Hague Congress of the First International sat from 2–7 September 1872. It was attended by sixty-five delegates, among whom were Marx and Engels. The powers of the General Council and the political activity of the proletariat were among the items on the agenda. The Congress deliberations were marked throughout by a sharp struggle against the Bakuninists. The Congress passed a resolution extending the General Council's powers. Its resolution 'On the Political Activity of the Proletariat' stated that the proletariat should organize a political party of its own to ensure the triumph of the social revolution and that the winning of political power was becoming its great task. The Congress expelled Bakunin and Guillaume from the International as disorganizers and founders of a new, anti-proletarian party.

2. *Zarya* (Dawn) – a Marxist scientific and political journal published in Stuttgart in 1901–2 by the editors of *Iskra*. Four issues appeared in three instalments.

3. The reference is to the Fifth World Congress of the Second International, which met in Paris from 23 to 27 September 1900. On the fundamental issue, 'The Winning of Political Power, and Alliances with Bourgeois Parties', whose discussion was prompted by A. Millerand becoming a member of the Waldeck-Rousseau counter-revolutionary government, the Congress carried a motion tabled by Kautsky. The resolution said that

'the entry of a single Socialist into a bourgeois Ministry cannot be considered as the normal beginning for winning political power: it can never be anything but a temporary and exceptional makeshift in an emergency situation'. Afterwards, opportunists frequently referred to this point to justify their collaboration with the bourgeoisie.

Zarya published (No. 1, April 1901) an article by Plekhanov entitled 'A Few Words About the Latest World Socialist Congress in Paris. An Open Letter to the Comrades Who Have Empowered Me', which sharply criticized Kautsky's resolution.

4. Pannekoek, Anton (1873–1960): Joined Dutch Social Democratic Workers Party [SDAP] in 1899; helped found De Tribune in 1907; expelled from SDAP and was a founding member of left-wing SDP in 1909, which became CP in 1918; theoretician of left-wing communism and of German KAPD; his current broke from Comintern in 1921; worked with ultra-left groups in Netherlands and the United States; prominent astronomer.

5. This refers to Sidney Webb and Beatrice Webb (1897), *Industrial Democracy*, vol. I (1 ed.), London, New York, Bombay: Longmans, Green & Co; Sidney Webb and Beatrice Webb (1897), *Industrial Democracy*, vol. II (1 ed.), London, New York, Bombay: Longmans, Green & Co.

Webb, Beatrice (1858–1943): English socialist and historian with husband, Sidney. Activist in socialist movements including the Fabians. Author of a series of historical works.

Webb, Sidney (1859–1947): A founder of Fabian Society; co-author with wife Beatrice of numerous books on cooperatives and trade unionism; became minister in 1924 of the Labour government. He and his wife became apologists for Stalinism in the 1930s.

6. Potresov, Aleksander Nikolalevich (1869–1934): A Founder of the Russian Social Democracy. Member of the Iskra Group; Menshevik. A close associate of Lenin but later broke with him. Also called Starover. Social-chauvinist during World War I. Active anti-Bolshevik in the Civil War. Emigrated 1922 to Paris.

7. Kolb, Wilhelm (1870–1918): Son of a shoemaker; Catholic, later without religious confession; attended elementary school in Karlsruhe; initially apprenticed as sculptor, then apprenticeship as a painter in Karlsruhe; journeyman in Germany and Switzerland; married in 1894; joined Social Democratic Party in 1891, trade union in 1888; worked as a (house) painter and whitewasher until 1894. Chairman of the Social Democratic party in the Landtag in Baden from 1905–18, long-serving chairman of party in Karlsruhe. Member of Landtag in Baden from 1905–18. Regular contributor to the revisionist Sozialistische Monatshefte, and author of a number of pamphlets (e.g. *Die Sozialdemokratie am Scheidewege*, 1905). Kolb was a

prominent advocate of reformist strategy and revisionism, and the leading protagonist of the Social Democratic Party's strategy of cross-class and cross-party collaboration at the state level in Baden.

8. *Soʒialistische Monatshefte* [The Socialist Monthly]: The principal journal of the opportunists among the German Social Democrats. It was published in Berlin from 1897 to 1933. During the world imperialist war of 1914–18, it took a social-chauvinist stand.

9. Turati, Filippo (1857–1932): Leader of the right wing of the Socialist Party, he sustained a polity of openness and co-operation with the bourgeoisie. Edited, together with Anna Kuliscioff, the review Critica sociale [Social Criticism]. In 1896 he became deputy. In 1903 Giolitti offered him to join the government. Although he wished to accept this proposal, he was compelled to refuse because of the internal opposition inside the socialist party. After the end of the First World War, while the party was expressing itself in favour of a more strict and constant relation with the Comintern, Turati worked to regain the dialogue with Giolitti. In 1922 his reformist wing splits from the Socialist Party, giving birth to the Unitarian Socialist Party of Italy [Partito Socialista Unitario Italiano].

Treves, Claudio (1868–1933): Italian socialist. Critic of Bolshevism.

10. The manuscript continues as follows:

Chapter VII: The Experience of the Russian Revolutions of 1905 and 1917

The subject indicated in the title of this chapter is so vast that volumes could be written about it. In the present pamphlet we shall have to confine ourselves, naturally, to the most important lessons provided by experience, those bearing directly upon the tasks of the proletariat in the revolution with regard to state power. [Here the manuscript breaks off – Ed.]